Peace Mom

Peace Mom

A Mother's Journey
Through Heartache to Activism

Cindy Sheehan

ATRIA BOOKS

New York   London   Toronto   Sydney

ATRIA BOOKS

1230 Avenue of the Americas
New York, NY 10020

Library of Congress Cataloging-in-Publication Data

Sheehan, Cindy.
Peace mom : a mother's journey through heartache to activism /
Cindy Sheehan.
p.   cm.
1. Iraq War, 2003—Protest movements—United States.
2. Sheehan, Cindy.   3. Sheehan, Casey Austin, 1979–2004.
4. Women pacifists—United States—Biography.
5. Pacifists—United States—Biography.   6. Mothers of war casualties—
United States—Biography.   7. Iraq War, 2003—Casualties.
8. Bush, George W. (George Walker), 1946– .   I. Title.
DS79.76.S533 2006
956.7044'31—dc22 [B]   2006050095

ISBN-13: 978-0-7432-9792-9

First Atria Books hardcover edition September 2006

1   3   5   7   9   10   8   6   4   2

ATRIA BOOKS is a trademark of Simon & Schuster, Inc.

Manufactured in the United States of America

For information about special discounts for bulk purchases,
please contact Simon & Schuster Special Sales:
1-800-456-6798 or business@simonandschuster.com.

*This book is dedicated to my three surviving children,
Carly, Andy, and Janey, who exhibit their courage, integrity,
and compassion every day. They are my living heroes,
to whose futures I dedicate my continuing work for peace.*

———————————

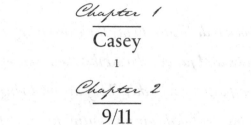

Contents

Foreword

I READ A POEM ABOUT A TOMBSTONE ONCE. THE POET described how the engraved birth date and death date tell about only two brief moments in time of the departed one's history.

According to the poet, the living happens in the dash between the dates.

This book is the story of Casey Austin Sheehan.

May 29, 1979–April 4, 2004.

This book is about Casey's dash. About his short but meaningful life and how it has inspired his mom to a lifelong quest for peace and justice, and how Casey's dash has inspired thousands of people to give meaning and fulfillment to their dashes.

This is also a story about my dash.

Cindy Lee Miller Sheehan

July 10, 1957–TBD

This book is the heartbreaking story of how my son Casey inspired me to give my dash meaning and to make him as proud of my life as I always was of his.

Casey started screaming the minute his head popped out of my birth canal at 1:01 A.M. on May 29, 1979. Looking back with hindsight, I know he didn't want to enter this "vale of tears," but he had to. He had a mission.

On May 29, 1979, I gave birth to my son. My darling boy. The old soul with the wise eyes that could penetrate my soul from the time those eyes opened.

I gave physical birth to Casey on that glorious day in May. On April 4, 2004, Casey died. He was killed in Iraq in an ambush by the al Sadr resistance fighters. He died going to rescue his buddies. He was shot in the back of the head while he was riding in the rear of a trailer in Sadr City, Baghdad.

I didn't know it then, but I know it now. When Casey died in that back alley of Baghdad, five days after he arrived "in country," he gave spiritual birth to his real mom. The real mom who was hiding behind her ignorance, faith, marriage, family, and comfort began to emerge on April 4.

As I lay in a crumpled heap screaming on the evening of April 4 after the merchants of death and doom came to my house to tell me my son was dead, something snapped. Something had to. No one can take that kind of physical and psychic pain without snapping.

The angels didn't take me that day. I now know as I was screaming "No, no, no! Not Casey, oh God, no!" over and over again, I made a choice and an agreement with the universe.

I had to decide something in my heart and soul. Would I stay here and fall into a depression of grief and regret? Would

I voluntarily leave and join Casey through suicide? Or would I stay and fight? At that moment, my soul chose to stay and fight.

How else can I explain the source of strength and courage that has poured into me and through me beginning with the awful moment I learned that he had been prematurely taken from me and our family?

Casey's life was and has been a source of that courage and strength.

This book is a celebration of Casey's extraordinary life.

This book is also an odyssey of one mom's journey from a place of pure pain to one of pain that is also infused with joy and hope.

This book is a story of one mom's journey from being a "normal" mom to one who went to the seat of power and challenged the king and triumphed and who meets and is lauded by heads of state and also vilified and hated by other heads of state and much of the American media.

This book is a story of one mom's journey from believing that her son was a "war hero" to believing that her son died as a victim of the war machine.

This is a book of one mom's journey from ignorance of history (even though, ironically, she majored in history) to being an active participant in making history and having an effect on social change.

This is a book of one mom's journey from trusting her leaders even when they so brazenly take our country to bogus war, to one of pacifism and nonviolence at all costs.

I hope you enjoy my book because, above all, this is a book about my journey from being an apathetic consumer of physical comforts and the American way to being an activist who struggles against physical comforts and the American way for violence and the military-industrial complex.

This book is also the love story between Casey and me and our love for humankind and peace. How our lives became intertwined with some amazing and good people, but how we also became enmeshed in the dark world of some very bad people.

This is my story of how one person can, should, and must make a difference. This is the incredible story of how I went from being Mom to four to being the "Peace Mom" to thousands.

The journey is in the dash.

I hope Casey's story and my story inspire you to expand your dash and infuse it with meaning, laughter, dancing, hope, love, and, most of all, life.

Chapter 1

Casey

"It's a boy!"
—Dr. Blum, May 29, 1979

*"You're looking at the newest recruit
in the United States Army."*
—Casey Sheehan, May 2000

WRITING THIS BOOK IS THE SECOND MOST DIFFICULT thing I have ever done, next to burying Casey. I sit here writing with a box of Kleenex by my side and a pile of used ones on the floor next to me.

This is the most difficult chapter to write.

Who knows when this story begins?

Does it start when I was born? No, I don't think my less-than-functional upbringing is too relevant to the story.

Does it begin when I met my husband of twenty-eight years, and my children's father, Pat? That would be a closer beginning and a little more pertinent to the story, but not close enough.

1

I think the true beginning of the story is when Casey was born. The unbreakable bond between Casey and me is the true foundation of what has subsequently occurred in our lives and the Super Glue that keeps me together and constantly working for peace no matter how hard the effort.

I always loved babies when I was growing up in Bellflower, a smallish suburb of Los Angeles. I was an extremely shy, introverted girl who had few friends except for my constant companion: books. I was reading at a college level when I was in fifth grade and loved to read more than anything else.

I was in constant demand as a baby-sitter in my neighborhood and by my parents' friends. I couldn't wait to "grow up," get married, and have children of my own.

I met my future husband, Patrick Sheehan, when I was sixteen years old, between my junior and senior years of high school. While I was growing up in Bellflower, Pat was growing up in the town next door, Norwalk. We were married in April 1977, when I was nineteen years old.

We were both ecstatic when we found out we were pregnant in 1978 with the little guy who would turn out to be Casey Austin.

We carefully chose the furniture that would last through all four of our children, and we painted and wallpapered the baby's bedroom in our tiny first home. The wallpaper was a Disney print that I'd had in my playhouse when I was growing up.

We attended childbirth classes and were determined that our new baby would be born as naturally as possible, without drugs, and that the baby would be nursed and I would quit my job to be a full-time mom to our child.

On the day before our eagerly anticipated baby was born, Pat and I attended an air show in Long Beach, California. We have a picture of me leaning up against a pier railing, standing sideways to show my big belly. I was wearing some dorky white maternity bathing-suit bottoms that were long like shorts, and a blue-and-white-checked, three-quarter-sleeve maternity top. My belly was sticking out as if I were getting ready to deliver a baby right then and there!

I was tan and fit-looking despite my big belly. I had left my job as a loan adjuster for Security Pacific National Bank a month before Casey was born and spent my days swimming at my gym. I loved swimming when I was pregnant with Casey. He was an unusually active baby in utero, even compared to my next three. He loved it when I swam, too. It was the only time, really, that he would lie still.

At the air show, Pat and I finally decided on a name for the baby. Our natural-childbirth instructor had a really cute son named Casey, and my family, on my mom's side, had a tradition of giving sons the middle name Austin. So, Casey Austin it was to be for a boy. We decided on Julie Anne for a girl. I'm not exactly sure why Julie, except when I was growing up my beloved maternal grandma made me a rag doll that I loved and named Julie, and Anne for my sister, and one of Pat's sisters had the middle name Anne. We were ready for the baby, who was due on June 5.

The next day, I went into labor. It was a fairly easy labor until about six that evening when my water broke and the contractions came faster and stronger. We were with Pat's sister Cherie, and we decided it was probably time to go to the hospital.

I was sitting on our couch, and Cherie and I were timing my contractions. Pat disappeared for a short while and reappeared with tools and a package. I asked him what in the name of God he was he doing.

He said, "I'm going to fix the toilet!"

I sat on the couch and roared with laughter between contractions. The toilet had been running and Pat had had the parts to fix it since we had moved into the house a year earlier, but he waited until my water broke to finally fix it!

After Pat was finished with his plumbing job, Cherie dropped him and me and the unborn one off at Kaiser Hospital, which was about two blocks from our house. During the next five hours, before Casey was born, about twenty friends and relatives gathered in the waiting room to await the birth of the first child of Pat and Cindy Sheehan.

I'll just skim through the gorier details of the labor: the hour of blowing through contractions when I had to push, because the nurses wouldn't come in and check me to see if I was ready to push; the two hours of pushing because I was so tired from blowing through an hour of contractions; the horribly botched episiotomy that caused me weeks of pain after Casey was born; or my locking myself in the bathroom in the labor room, almost causing Pat to faint in his heightened state of anxiety.

What I will regale you with is the birth of my eight-pound, two-ounce, twenty-one-and-a-half-inch-long perfect son, who started screaming as soon as his mouth hit the atmosphere of his new world. He was put to my breast immediately and calmed right down. I swear he looked at me before the nurse whisked him away to clean him up and take his vitals; he looked at me, and we immediately knew each other.

Casey, Pat, and I became the inseparable threesome that did everything together. My schedule revolved around Casey. We sat up late at night in the rocking chair that my dad, Grandpa Miller, bought us, watching old movies, singing, playing patty-cake, and staring at each other with love. I'd beg Casey to go to sleep, and Casey would finally comply around 3 or 4 A.M.; we were always awake together, or asleep together.

To get a little housework done, sometimes I would sit him in his car seat on a surface close to me. Often he would stare up at the ceiling and just jabber away happily at something. I always said he was talking to his angels. He was such a good baby. When he awakened each morning he would lie in his crib and talk to his angels, or play with the toys in the crib for at least an hour so I could slowly wake up before he would demand that I come in and get him so he could have his best friend, me, to play with.

"Mamaaaaaaa, Mamaaaaaaaaa," he would call from his crib. If I didn't answer, he would call to Pat: "Dadaaaaaaa. Dadaaaaaa!"

Recently we sadly commemorated the second anniversary of Casey's murder in Iraq. His brother, sisters, Auntie, and my best friend, Liz, were standing around his grave shivering in the cold wind, and the dark clouds were filled with rain, which was very unusual in Vacaville for April. We were recounting memories of Casey.

Auntie, my sister, went first. She recalled how as a toddler Casey loved to pull every book that I owned out of the bookcase and throw them into piles on the floor. Soon after he taught himself that little game, I instructed him not to do it. After that, he would crawl up to the bookcase, pull himself up by one of the shelves, and stretch out his hand to the books but would never touch one. He would shake his head and say "Book. No! No!" over and over again.

Carly Anne, now twenty-five and drop-dead gorgeous with her lithe body, long shining hair, and teeth that only thousands of dollars of orthodontia could produce, used to be my oldest daughter. Now she is my oldest child. Which is not right—there are four Sheehan children, not three, and the oldest should be a boy! Carly recounted how, when Casey was seven and studying for his First Holy Communion, they began to "play mass." All of the kids would gather in Carly's room, pull her nightstand away from the wall, put a dish towel on it, and use Wheat Thins for communion wafers. Of course, Casey would always be the priest.

Janey, my baby, my doll, is now twenty and was a senior in high school just starting her last spring break before graduating when her brother was killed. He was so sad that he would have to miss her graduation because he would be over in Iraq. She told about how she and her best friend, Janae, would always irritate Casey while he was playing a video game until he got up and roared and chased them around the house.

Andy, my youngest son, who is now my only son, was so choked up he couldn't speak. Andy was five years Casey's junior and is now twenty-two. He looks more and more like his brother every day. He is now a land surveyor who is about six feet two inches tall with a sturdy but lean build. One day I walked into our living room. Andy was asleep on the couch and he looked so much like Casey, my heart skipped more than a few beats. I remember Andy gave a comment to one of the television crews who were camped out on the street by our church, St. Mary's, before Casey's Rosary service. He said, "How do you think I feel? I have lost my only brother."

My friend Liz remembered all of the times that we watched pay-per-view wrestling events together. Casey was such a huge fan of professional wrestling, which he called "soap operas for guys." But sadly, I am not convinced that he knew it was fake, even up until the end. I remember watching with Casey a WWE event broadcast from Baghdad during the last Christmas he was home, and he was so thrilled to think that the WWE might come back to Iraq the next Christmas, when he was going to be there. Tragically, my boy didn't even make it to Easter.

The memory I shared of Casey was when it was just we two. We played together, took walks together, napped together, went grocery shopping together, frequently visited Auntie at her "May-mart" (Kmart, where she was the personnel manager). Casey was the favorite May-mart baby and was spoiled and loved by everyone who worked there. I had his picture taken once a month by the in-store photographer.

About once a day, when I would be doing dishes, or cooking, Casey would walk up to me and say, "Doyun, huh Mama?" which meant "What are you doing, Mama?" I would say, "I'm cooking dinner, Casey." And he would then wrap his arms around my legs, kiss me on my behind, and say, "I wuv you, Mama!" I would pick him up and cover his sweet, round face with kisses and say, "I wuv you, Casey!" I would put him down and he would run off to whatever adventure he was getting into at the time.

Since I gave birth to my younger three at home with midwives, Casey was present for all of their births. One of the reasons I decided to have Carly at home was so that I wouldn't have to leave Casey for a day or two while I was in the hospital. I didn't want him to have any separation anxiety and blame the new baby for his mama being gone from him.

While I was in labor with Carly, many of our friends and relatives came in and out of my bedroom to take pictures, and a sister-in-law was filming the birth. Casey would come in every once in a while, holding his Fisher-Price camera, and he would tell me, "Say cheese, Mama." I would say "cheese" and he would "take" my picture and then go back out to be adored by various aunts, uncles, grandmas, and grandpas.

Despite all of our precautions against sibling rivalry, Casey did have one moment of it just a few hours after Carly was born. Pat and I were sitting on our bed, and I was nursing Carly. Casey wanted to get out of his crib, so Pat went and got him and Casey crawled up next to Carly and me. He was staring raptly at Carly nursing, and I was wondering if he remembered when he used to do that. He was rubbing her head really gently and saying "Nice baby, nice baby," when all of a sudden he smacked her little head. I pushed him back onto the bed and said, "No, no, she is your sister, be nice!" Then I had two crying babies on my hands!

The next five years went by in a blur of births, babies, breasts, diapers, and bleary-eyed midnight feedings, and it seemed that for those five years I always had two in diapers, or in various stages of potty-training. Since we used cloth diapers and we had four young "tinklers," my washing machine was always going and we wore out several motors. I also remember that as the time when my couch was always piled high with laundry that needed to be folded.

Pat had a game with the kids that he would play to get them to put away the clothes. They would have races doing various activities. He would hand them all a pile of clothes to be put away and would instruct them to "hop on one foot" or "hop like bunnies" or another activity and they would have so much fun they didn't even know they were doing chores.

I always tried to keep a clean home, free of as many nasty germs as possible, but we also wanted our kids to have fun in their home. They would run the length of our coffee table and jump into our arms, or into a chair. I would enter our long hallway where all the bedrooms are and I would find one or more of them "spider" walking up the walls. One morning we decided we'd had enough pancakes, so we used them as Frisbees and soared them all over the kitchen. We had a fun life, even if it sometimes approached total anarchy in our house.

One thing that was sacred to Pat and me was bath- and bedtime. Our kids had a strict bedtime of 8 P.M., and we would tuck them in and individually tell them stories or talk about their days with them before kissing them good night and collapsing on the couch together to watch some TV before we exhaustedly fell asleep, too—many times right on the couch!

Casey had a thing he would say every night when we tucked him in, and it is so heartbreaking to remember it. We would sit on his bed and talk about his day and before we kissed him he would say, "Thank you, Mom and Dad, this was the best day of my life." He had such a sweet soul that was brimming with love. He was so even-tempered and exuded an otherworldly peace his entire life. We would joke around and say he was in his "Casey universe" when sometimes he would be zoned out or deep in concentration. I wish I had asked him what he was thinking about. He always had one foot in this world and one foot in the next. It was as if he never really belonged fully to us or the planet Earth.

Imagine our shock and surprise when he came home from a long day away when he was twenty-one in the spring of 2000 and announced to us, "You're looking at the newest recruit in the United States Army." When I asked him why he had joined the Army, he said something strange that I never really thought about until he died. He said, "I thought I was supposed to." He looked briefly confused when he said that. Who told him he was "supposed to"? How did he know that? His dad and I certainly never told him to join the Army.

Since we lived near Travis Air Force Base, in Fairfield, Casey had been actively recruited to join the Air Force since he was a junior in high school. He always said no, and the recruiter would go on his way.

One time I came home from work to find Casey sitting in the living room with a gentleman in a uniform. Casey was bent over the table taking some kind of a test. After the sergeant left, I asked Casey what that was all about. That's when he informed me he was thinking about joining the Army. The Army! "Why, Casey?"

"Well, I can finish college in the Army, I can be a chaplain's assistant, and they will give me a twenty-thousand-dollar signing bonus," he proudly said. I wondered whether he wanted to give up four years of his life for this.

The next day he disappeared all day to take more tests. Lickety-split, before we could even talk him out of it, he had enlisted.

Casey went into the Army on the DEP: Delayed Entry Program. He needed to finish one more class in the summer, and he was planning on a trip to Rome for the Catholic World Youth

Day celebration in August. He was scheduled to go to boot camp on August 31. We didn't know at that time that we had recourse: People who go into the service on the DEP can get out of it right up until the time they report for boot camp. I wish to God we had known that. I think we could have talked him out of it, but we thought it was a done deal.

As for the promises that his recruiter made to him, he broke every single one. Not many people know that the enlistment contract is only binding on the recruit and not on the government. Such unilateral contracts are not even legal, and our young people are being trapped into situations that they were lied into. Casey never got one thing he was promised by his recruiter. But the only promise I care about is the one that his recruiter made promising him that he would never see combat. He was killed in combat five days after he went to Iraq.

Our families were not military families. Pat's dad was in the Navy in World War II and my dad was in the Army between wars in the fifties. They both did their stints and then got out to civilian life. Pat tried to enlist in the Air Force during Vietnam because he had a low lottery number, but he had high blood pressure and he wasn't able to enlist. I bet his mother sobbed with joy! With five hundred to six hundred of our boys coming home in flag-draped coffins every week during that conflict, any mother in her right mind would want her child to avoid going to that wrong war. But my mother-in-law, although devastated by Casey's death, believes in George Bush and this insanity in Iraq. She does believe that Casey died for a "noble cause." I wonder how she would have felt if Pat had died? I can only speculate.

Looking back on Casey's life, I realize that I did some very wrong things with him, thinking they were the right things.

I put him and our other children in Catholic schools because our public schools in Norwalk were so horrible. He was subjected to abusive nuns who tried to strip away every ounce of individuality that he had. One of Casey's elementary school teachers was a nun who, I found out much later, hit her students! I am sure that there are many good Catholic schools out there, but my kids went to ones that were run like little fascist regimes. I have since left the misogynistic and superstitious church, and I have come to feel distrustful of most organized religion.

Too often, organized religion tries to brainwash us into thinking that our religion is the only one that is right, and if someone is not of our particular religion, then he or she must be going to Hell. If you are not a member of my religion, then it must be okay for my leaders to send troops to kill you. Fundamentalists of all religions are responsible for the astounding mess we are in right now. Whether they are Christian crazies, Muslim extremists, or Zionist Jews, the leaders of these factions love nothing more than to whip up their followers into a frenzy of hate and fear against those who believe differently.

Another mistake I made was to invest so much of our lives

and my children's lives in Scouting. I've come to believe that the Boy Scouts is just another organization that trains young men to be "good soldiers." Casey eventually attained the rank of Eagle and we were so proud of all of his Boy Scout badges, but Scouting is just a natural ingress into the world of the military. As an adult, Casey was proud to earn his "man scout" badges when he was a soldier. I was even given a taste of this when I was pinned with my Gold Star after Casey was killed. The Gold Star mom who pinned me lost two sons in Vietnam—and she acted as if I should be thrilled with the honor of having that badge pinned on me.

I had already decided by then, even in my deep shock and absolute pain, that I wasn't going to be a "good scout." I was going to fight against the idea that dying for a piece of cloth with stripes on it to spread a failed idea of freedom and democracy was worth it. A Gold Star is not a fair trade for a son's life.

Yes, I made mistakes in Casey's life, but they were made out of love and my brainwashing as a good scout.

Now, through Casey's sacrifice and my reversal of the brainwashing that led to his death—I guess you could say my brain got dirty again—we two pals for life are waking this country up and getting its citizens' minds out of the false-patriotism gutter, making a new world where it is *not* okay to fight, kill, and perhaps die to earn your good-scout badges.

It is wrong. We paid dearly for the lies.

May 29, 1979, was the happiest day of my life. I will never

forget the day that true joy came into my life and the true hope that came from giving birth to a perfect angel.

April 4, 2004, was the worst day of my life and I thought hope was extinguished that day, but Casey's true mom was born as Casey became a real angel.

Chapter 2

9/11

*"Mom, come here! A plane just crashed into
one of the World Trade towers!"*
—CARLY SHEEHAN, MORNING OF SEPTEMBER 11, 2001

I STILL REMEMBER THE DREAM I HAD ON THE MORN-
ing of September 11, 2001. I am lovingly setting a very delicate
crystal vase that I have just cleaned on the back of the toilet in
the front bathroom. As I am leaning over with the beautiful
piece of fine crystal in my hands, the vase slips from my hands
and shatters into a million pieces all over the toilet bowl! The
vase explodes into my face and eyes and I feel like I've been pep-
pered with shotgun pellets.

Great, I think to myself as the blood trickles onto the bathroom floor, *now I'll have to go to the hospital and get these pieces of
glass picked out of my face.* I know I'm in for a long day waiting in
ER lines and wasting my time.

The scene shifts, and now I am being hauled out of my
youth ministry office at St. Mary's Catholic Church. I am cough-

ing and gagging on smoke and covered with black soot. A fireman who is also covered in black soot is dragging me to safety.

"Mom, come here!"

I was jerked awake from my nightmare by the sound of my daughter Carly screaming from the converted family room that had become her bedroom in our tiny home.

I ran into her room and saw her sitting cross-legged on her bed with tears streaming down her face, staring at the small TV on her dresser. "A plane just crashed into one of the World Trade towers!" My knees gave out and I sat on the bed with Carly as we watched in horror as the real nightmare events of that day unfolded. It was such a gorgeous day in New York City, and across the country in California, we were also experiencing one of our trademark beautiful early-fall days.

What a contrast to the ugliness and terror that we were all feeling. The day of 9/11 and the following days were absolutely beautiful, but as the towers crumbled and as the rubble smoldered, our lives and our psyches as American citizens who believed we were basically safe and morally sound were also crumbling and smoldering.

The nightmare that I had on the morning of September 11, 2001, was just the culmination of some terrible yet vague feelings of unease that I was having before the event. In the weeks leading up to 9/11, there were many reported shark attacks off America's shores and a few fathers in the hinterlands went berserk and killed their entire families and then themselves. I thought that the disturbed sharks and the disturbed people were feeling some kind of disturbance in the force, if you will, and were acting accordingly. I felt as if there was some kind of universal pressure amassing and something was about to snap.

And then came 9/11. Thus began one of the most tragic and horrible experiences that we as citizens of the United States of America have ever had to go through as a fairly young (in the scheme of things) nation.

As a nation, we all shared the experience of the next days, weeks, and months as we collectively tried to make sense of the worst day in recent history. We all walked around with dazed looks on our faces—sort of zombielike in our appearance and in our souls. It was too horrible to feel at that point. Shock is a valuable tool. Shock gets you through the worst times.

For the first time in my life I sent money to the Red Cross and watched cable news networks around the clock. For some reason, Aaron Brown comforted me. Just knowing the Clark Kent–like reporter was still on the job gave me a sense of stability that I, rightly or wrongly, clung to.

We all mourned the human losses. But more than that, we mourned the loss of our national naïveté. To call what we were experiencing "mourning" seems very shallow and insufficient for the depth of sorrow, confusion, and anxiety that we were all feeling.

We were attacked! America was attacked on its own soil. We reeled with the implications of that. Our heads spun with grief and our souls melted in shock.

How could this happen? How could such a fuckup on such a

massive scale happen? Didn't we as a nation spend billions of dollars every year on national defense? Didn't we have the most powerful military in human history? Yes, we did.

The US of A spends far more on defense than all of the other nations of the world combined. More than 50 percent of our GNP goes to the defense budget every year. Bush just recently stated that he wanted to add another 125 nukes to our already obscene arsenal. Why do we need more nukes? Well, call me cynical, but I believe he has some buddies in the "nucular" bomb industry who want a bigger piece of the defense pie.

A fat lot of good all of our defense spending did us on 9/11. We felt weak, vulnerable, and, most of all, frightened. We felt very un-American. After all, the entire paradigm of American strength and invincibility went down the drain with the collapse of two towers and a hole in the Pentagon.

No wonder we were so easily led down the path to more destruction by the Bush regime. No wonder we gave him and his neocon minions carte blanche to recklessly lead us into two wars against two innocent countries that had nothing to do with the criminal act perpetrated on innocent Americans on 9/11.

I realize that many people who disagree with the Iraq war and have disagreed with it from the start think that the invasion of Afghanistan was justified. I never believed that. Even if we did believe that Osama was hiding there, it did not give the United States and coalition forces the right to invade an innocent country that had nothing to do with the horror of 9/11.

We will never get over the dreadfulness of 9/11—but it was

a criminal act perpetrated on America by a few criminals. It was not an act of war. Pearl Harbor was an act of war. On December 7, 1941, we were attacked by a country that had a defined border and an army that wore uniforms.

I personally know many families who had loved ones killed on that tragic day of 9/11 who did not want two countries filled with innocent people devastated because their loved ones were killed by criminals. More innocent Afghans were killed in the initial invasion of Afghanistan than Americans were killed on 9/11. When is enough killing enough? When are our pounds of flesh repaid? How much innocent blood must be shed? Even if we stipulate that the invasion of 9/11 was about vengeance, when have we exacted enough?

Juan Torres, a member of Gold Star Families for Peace, a group that I helped found, had a son killed in Afghanistan. Juan is an immigrant to the United States from Argentina. He calls his handsome son, John, his "American Dream." John was deployed to Afghanistan in 2004.

On July 12, 2004, my dear friend's son, John, was killed in a shower on his post. Juan was told that John had committed suicide by shooting himself, but subsequent investigations have shown that John was hit in the back of the head with a baseball bat and killed by a fellow soldier. John had been sending back e-mails and making phone calls complaining to his father about the drug trade on his post. Juan believes this is why John was killed.

Now that the United States has devastated Afghanistan,

even more than before, the country is back in the hands of the warlords and producing more opium than ever. The only half-way safe place in the entire country is Kabul.

All one has to do is look at the puppet government headed up by President Karzai to understand that the United States needed to take Afghanistan first to provide access to the land to build a pipeline for Iraq's oil, because the only other way through to the gulf was via Iran, and we all know that wouldn't have been possible.

We as Americans abdicated our responsibility to be a source of checks and balances on our government. We lost our healthy skepticism of government when we lost our innocence on 9/11.

We blindly followed leaders into Hell because they could climb up on a rubble pile and demonstrate that they could use a bullhorn. We allowed them to spread their cancer of Pax Americana because we were told that the best thing we could do after 9/11 was to go shopping and to travel. Shopping and travel?! Excellent, we love to shop and travel!

On top of our national grief, shock, and worry there were also the personal, human tragedies of that day. We looked at the pictures of the many missing citizens from the World Trade Center towers and we heard stories of courage and compassion.

I could barely watch my TV screen and see the walls covered with the hundreds of pictures of missing loved ones: "Have you seen this person?" On the morning of 9/11, I watched in horror and grief as one after another, the firefighters and police officers ran back into the towers to try to help the occupants escape. I feared that many of them would not come out alive.

As a mother whose world revolved around her children, the personal stories of loss on 9/11 depressed me even more.

I could fully sympathize, but not empathize, with the people whose loved ones had been killed. Such a tragedy had never unfolded in my own life. How could I know what these mothers were going through? But I did know one thing. They were living my worst nightmare as a mother: having a child die before I did.

My dad died in February of 1994, and that was a hard time in my life. And my father was not the best father; he was an abusive alcoholic who died prematurely at the age of sixty from cancer all through his body. Of course, burying a parent is difficult, but burying your child is unspeakable and disordered.

The surviving family members of 9/11 didn't even have the partial closure of having a body to bury; their loved ones were buried in a pile of rubble.

The terrorist attacks on 9/11 shocked and dismayed me and sent me into a depression from which I would never fully recover. Somehow, I knew that 9/11 would be the cause of Casey's death. I knew in my heart that the events of that day would have horrible implications for my family and for the world. I just didn't fully realize how horrible they would be.

I didn't hear from Casey for two days after the attacks. I was calling his cell phone about every half hour, frantic with worry. He was stationed in Killeen, Texas, at Fort Hood, and I knew that Casey's unit, the First Cavalry, was often the first unit to be sent off to war.

Not only was I concerned about all of the mothers and families of the dead, but I had a personal worry. Still trying to process the devastation of that day, I had a personal stake.

I couldn't eat. I couldn't sleep. I couldn't concentrate. I couldn't stop crying.

"Hi, Mom." What blessed words! Casey finally called on September 13. His voice sounded weary, but he was okay. My boy was okay.

His post had been put on high alert and they were very busy. He worked all day and fell into bed too exhausted to call at the end of each day.

I was crying with relief as we talked about 9/11. Casey had already heard some scuttlebutt that his unit might be going into Afghanistan. I was beside myself with grief and worry, but I tried to be as optimistic as I could so Casey wouldn't have to worry about his family on top of everything else.

Casey called me every day from Fort Hood when he wasn't training in the field. We would chat about what his brother and sisters were up to, what was going on in Vacaville and at the Youth Group, even what the dogs were doing. Sometimes we just listened to each other breathe. Casey wasn't the best conversationalist, but I know he called on a daily basis to feel connected with his family and with me. So I always tried to put the best face on everything and tried to make him feel like he was a part of everything.

I treasured those phone calls. They always came around 4 or 5 P.M., which would have been 6 or 7 P.M. in Texas. It took me almost a year after Casey was killed to stop thinking "Oh, maybe that's Casey" when the phone rang, especially at his special time. My heart would skip a beat and then I would cry for the emptiness and the loss.

I talk to so many moms in the same situation, and we all have the same experience. It is so hard to believe that your soldier boy is never coming home because he has been gone for so long already. It is hard to believe that he won't come home on leave soon; call when he can; send a letter or e-mail . . . when those letters and e-mails don't come, when your soldier boy doesn't call or come home for leave, the reality sinks in and sends you into another tailspin of grief and pain.

I am convinced that my nightmare on the morning of 9/11 was a premonition of the nightmare path that we as a nation and we as the Sheehan family were about to embark on—what a slippery slope to disaster George Bush was about to lead our nation down.

I often think of the dream that I had before I awoke to a more terrible reality that morning of the collapse of our innocence.

Did the vase represent life in all of its beauty and fragility? Did the fireman represent Casey who in a relatively short time would rescue his buddies and lead his mom onto a path of activism and out of the apathy that had marked her life up until that point?

My premonition that the events of 9/11 would be the death of Casey would come true three and a half years later. The true irony is that while it had everything to do with Casey's death, 9/11 also had nothing to do with Casey's death.

Our "leaders" started the biggest smear campaign against Saddam Hussein and Iraq that has ever been foisted on America and the world. The tail was about to wag the dog and we were about to be sold a bill of goods that would cost my family an inestimable price. The humanity of every American was about to be challenged.

These were America's darkest days and our government failed us miserably.

And we allowed our government to fail us.

Chapter 3

Rush to Disaster

*"Oh, well, how much damage can this
idiot do in four years?"*
—CINDY SHEEHAN AFTER GEORGE'S SELECTION
BY THE SUPREME COURT IN 2000

THE ABOVE QUOTE WAS THE MOST IRONIC THOUGHT
that I have ever had in my entire life! If I'd had even a small premonition of the damage that our new president would do to the
world, to America, and to my family, maybe I would have
fought harder against his selection. Not opposing him with
every fiber of my being will probably turn out to be the biggest
regret of my life, because such apathy led to the death of my son.

The presidency of George W. Bush and my soon-to-be-
intimate link with him did begin innocently enough. I had
never heard the term *neocon* and I had never heard of such people
as Condi, Rummy, Dick, John Ashcroft, et al.

I was slightly amused when John Ashcroft covered the
breasts of the statues in the Justice Department with eight

thousand dollars' worth of drapery, but I was not alarmed. I think I was more pissed about the money than about what the covering up really represented: It meant cover-ups and deceit and the sinister path on which the religious right had put our country. The covering of the statues meant stunning hypocrisy. Hiding breasts was a perfect metaphor for the secrecy and duplicity that has characterized this administration from the beginning.

I was annoyed at all the vacations that George was taking at his Crawford, Texas, ranch. I didn't even know where Crawford was, but Casey told me that it wasn't too far from Fort Hood, and once in a while George would chopper in on Marine One and attend religious services on post.

I thought George Bush was an idiot, but a harmless one. The worst thing we had to face about him before 9/11 was his butchery of the English language. I did not like George Bush, but I falsely and catastrophically believed that he would serve out his four years and not be reelected. I paid dearly for my failure to become a better-informed citizen.

I didn't know that eggs had been thrown at George and Laura and their motorcade during the inauguration parade until I saw the footage in Michael Moore's movie *Fahrenheit 9/11*.

I'd never heard of the Project for the New American Century (PNAC) until after my son was killed for its agenda. In one of its documents regarding the desired building up of American defenses, PNAC says that a "Pearl Harbor–like event" will be required if their goals are going to be achieved quickly.

I did not know that when George Bush was still governor of Texas, he was telling his biographer that he wanted to be a "great war president" and that if he could invade Iraq he wouldn't "squander" his political capital as his father had.

Before George received the Republican nomination for the presidency in 2000, I didn't know that as governor of Texas he routinely abrogated his gubernatorial responsibility to review each capital murder case to a one-page summary (prepared by future U.S. attorney general Alberto Gonzales), or that he despicably had even mentally retarded citizens executed.

I didn't know that George Bush had been handed a daily intelligence briefing that specifically warned about an airplane attack in America while he was on his monthlong vacation in Crawford in the August before 9/11. I certainly didn't know that his August vacations were sacred to him and that four years later I would be doing my best to ruin one of them.

What action would I have taken if I had informed myself and been aware of my surroundings? What would I have done if I knew all of the things then that I know now?

I often contemplate the "baby Hitler scenario" when I think of George Bush. It's the time-machine fantasy. If I had a time machine (it always looks like H. G. Wells's invention), and if I rode in it back to the time when George Bush was a baby, could I kill him and save my son's life and the life of so many other people? I always come to the same conclusion: No. I couldn't kill anyone, not even a monster.

My feelings about George Bush have metamorphosed from

mild amusement, to wonder at his stupidity, to horrid shock, to contempt, to pity, and even to loathing.

I readily admit to all of those feelings I've had about our pretender to the Oval Office, but you may be surprised to learn that one feeling I had for him for a few minutes back in 2001 was admiration. I thought, at first, that he showed some strong leadership after 9/11 and was impressed with his calmness in the face of tragedy. Even after he lingered over *My Pet Goat* and went for a coward's ride all over the United States, I thought that by the next day he had recovered nicely. Besides, such a thing had never happened in the United States before, so how was a president supposed to act?

I am now free of any kind of admiration or respect for George Bush and his band of unmerry men and women. I believe if Al Gore had been able to take his rightful place as our president in 2000, he would not have reacted inappropriately to the events of 9/11. I can't say for sure, but I have this mother's feeling in my heart that Casey and many others would still be alive.

Well, enough of the daydreaming. Alas, our president is not Al Gore, but George W. Bush.

After George's couple of days of strength, his political capital started to be wasted with me. He began exploiting our fears and vulnerability by contemptibly linking Saddam Hussein with 9/11 and telling us that Saddam had weapons of mass destruction and that such weapons could be delivered by drone to the East Coast of the United States within forty-five minutes from Iraq. I howled with laughter when I heard that one. I never bought into this scenario of impending invasions and disaster. If Saddam had such capabilities, how come he'd never exercised them in the decade since the first Gulf War? If he hated our "freedom and democracy" so much, why didn't he go on the offensive years earlier when his country was being devastated by the U.N.-U.S.–led sanctions against his country? Anyone who still had his head screwed on correctly could see that these people were selling us a bill of goods.

In gathering his Coalition of the Willing, he began to smear such countries as France and Germany, who would not go along with his killing policies. George iterated over and over again, "You're either with us or against us." We all should have been against him. I was proud of Germany and France for standing up to such cowboy-macho blustering and bullying.

I admit, at this point, I began to slowly awaken from my slumber of the Clinton years. After eight years of scandal and corporate rule during the Reagan administration, I think I was ready for a little numbness in the seemingly halcyon years of Clinton . . . heck, a little semen on a blue dress didn't bother me at all. A little prosperity and peace seemed like a great respite after Reagan and Star Wars. Having an articulate and bright president was also a nice contrast to Ronnie. Now I long for the archconservatism of a Reagan compared to the neoconservatism of a Bush.

I started to awaken from my slumber for one reason: Casey. I knew Casey and his buddies were about to be used as pawns for

George and his buddies. I could see the rhetoric building up for military action in Iraq. Casey and the First Cav had dodged the bullet of Afghanistan. But my heart was aching for the mothers of those soldiers who had been deployed into the dangerous and unstable country of Afghanistan looking for one man who may or may not have even been hiding there.

I distinctly remember one scorching hot day in August up in the Gold Country of California.

Pat and I had stayed in a hotel in Oroville after a concert we had attended in Marysville. It was Jackson Browne and Tom Petty, two of our favorite artists. After the concert we had headed up to Oroville to visit Fr. Benedict DeLeon, who had been the pastor of St. Mary's in Vacaville during the years that I had worked there.

The best "job" I ever had in my entire life, besides being a peace activist, was as coordinator of youth ministry for St. Mary's. We had a highly successful youth ministry, the largest and most active in the entire Sacramento Diocese.

In my job as youth minister I was in charge of all activities and continuing religious education of the teens in our parish. Our group went on trips all over the country to youth conventions and did fun things such as our annual waterskiing trip to Collins Lake in Northern California. I formed so many bonds with the young people and their families. However, the best thing about the job was that my own children were involved in the ministry and I got to spend all of my time with them, even at work.

I did that job for seven years, very successfully, until our parish was assigned a new priest. Our old pastor, and a good friend of mine, Father DeLeon, had been very supportive of our ministry and of me, but our new pastor seemed hostile toward the youth and toward paying me to be their minister. I don't know why. I think it was about the money, but I am not sure.

This new pastor went on a campaign to destroy my credibility throughout the parish, and he was successful in some circles, less successful in others, and for an entire year tried to make me quit. I finally went into his office and told him that I loved my job and if he wanted me gone he was going to have to fire me. You see, I have a long history of standing up to the so-called power elite and for the people, such as my teens at the parish. I believe the horrible experience I had before the pastor finally did fire me prepared me for the neocon attack on my credibility during Camp Casey. But since Casey was killed, I have been fighting for the young people all over the world.

I remember being tan and fit that summer after I had been fired from my job as youth minister. I had two months' severance pay and I was working out and swimming every day. I felt healthy, but I was depressed over my firing, 9/11 still weighed heavily on my soul, and I was, of course, worried about Casey, who was still stationed at Fort Hood, and about the world. The summer of 2002 should have been the "Summer of Cindy," but I was depressed and in therapy.

Anyway, as Pat and I sat in the breakfast area of the Days Inn on that sunny and hot Sunday morning, CNN was on in the dining area. I watched the foreign minister of Iraq, Tariq Aziz, being interviewed. He said something that sent shivers up my spine and fear into my soul: "It doesn't matter what we do, you are going to invade our country anyway."

I knew that Mr. Aziz was correct. I could see that the U.N. weapons inspectors were saying that Saddam had no WMD.

I could smell something fishy when then Secretary of State Colin Powell was pointing at maps at the U.N. I could certainly smell something extremely fishy when Rummy was also pointing at areas on the map where Saddam had hidden WMD. How did Rummy know where they were? Did he help Saddam bury them?

I also remember another "joke" going around at the time:

Question: How does George Bush know that Saddam has WMD?

Answer: He kept the receipts.

I could tell that George and Co. were lying through their collective teeth in the lead-up to the invasion of Iraq. I, a mother/housewife from Vacaville, California, knew there was something rotten in the state of BushWorld . . . why couldn't everyone else see this?

I knew that something was wrong because of past history. If Saddam hated the United States and possessed the capability to use WMD against us, why hadn't he? I came up with two answers: He didn't use WMD against our country because he didn't have them *or* he didn't use WMD against the United

States because he knew it would be a disaster for him. It's the same reason that other countries don't use WMD on the United States . . . they know that our WMD are better and stronger than theirs and we could wipe their countries off the face of the earth.

I knew all this, and I had my suspicions about Bush and the chorus of doom, but did I do anything? Did I write any letters? Did I protest? Did I shout from the tops of the roofs all that I knew and suspected? No. Why? Why didn't I try to save Casey's life before it was taken?

One simple reason: I was praying that calm heads would prevail and that there would be no invasion of Iraq. I also, foolishly, believed that one person couldn't make a difference.

I found out that no matter how long one spends in prayer for peace, and no matter how long one kneels in desperate prayer trying to send protection vibes to one's soldier boy in a combat zone, praying doesn't work.

I will regret for the rest of my life that I didn't take action in the lead-up to the invasion. That I sat in my depression praying ineffectually and hoping against hope that reason would triumph.

I learned my lesson the hardest way a mother should ever have to.

In spite of all my praying, supplications, bargains with God, hoping, wishing, crying, and screaming, George Bush invaded Iraq anyway. His "shock and awe" campaign was aptly named. I was shocked that I allowed him to do something so stupid and shortsighted. I ultimately allowed him to kill my child.

Casey left for Kuwait on March 19, 2004. He was there for about two weeks before his unit convoyed to Iraq.

One of my motivations for the odyssey that I set upon after Casey was killed was to seek contrition for my mistake of a lifetime.

Mea culpa. Mea maxima culpa. I am sorry, Casey. I am sorry, world. I promise to do better.

Chapter 4

April 4, 2004

The Day Casey and I Died

"We regret to inform you . . ."
—GRIM REAPER, APRIL 4, 2004

I WOKE UP AROUND 9 A.M. ON 04/04/04, PALM SUN-day, a day I would later learn was the thirty-sixth anniversary of Martin Luther King Jr.'s assassination.

It was a gorgeous, and when I now reflect on it, achingly beautiful Northern California morning, and my neighbor was mowing his lawn in the bright sunshine. It was the first day in weeks, ever since Casey had shipped out to Iraq as a specialist mechanic, that I had awakened without a sense of impending doom. I knew that the war in Iraq did not have distinct battle zones, that every place Americans were stationed there was dangerous, but for once I thought, *He's in the motor pool, he's not in a combat unit; maybe I can relax a little and enjoy this wonderful day.*

Midmorning I went out to brunch with my friend Lynda.

We had not had time to see each other lately because I had recently gotten a new job working for Napa County, which meant two hours commuting every day between Vacaville and the city of Napa. Lynda and I had very different political views, but that was just something we agreed to disagree about. We didn't let it get in the way of our friendship, at least not until after Casey was killed, and that morning we had a great time together. We drank mimosas and promised that we would stay in closer contact.

After brunch I went grocery shopping and splurged on filet mignon to grill for dinner for Pat and me. Our three other children would not be there. Our son Andy was living on his own, and our daughters, Carly and Janey, would both be working.

We were a very close-knit family, and until Casey went into the Army and the other kids' schedules got too difficult to coordinate, we all ate dinner together every night. We'd talk about how the day had gone for each of us and trade opinions on current events. And we'd laugh. The kids could always break each other up with a joke or a wisecrack, and occasionally we pissed off Pat—who could be quite the serious dad—with burping and farting contests.

I missed those times when we were all together. Money was always tight and we had our struggles like every other family, but our house was filled with love. Now the kids were all grown, and it was natural that they had their own things to do.

Until dinner that Sunday, I did normal Sunday things. I

did laundry and got my clothes ready for the workweek. I cleaned house and puttered around. Carly and I had a nice long talk about a concert she had gone to the previous evening. I felt happy, as if a weight had been lifted off my shoulders.

While I was preparing dinner, I remembered that in February, shortly after I got my new job, I had told Carly that I thought 2004 was going to be a great year for our family, and that the only thing that could ruin it would be if something happened to Casey in Iraq. That brought up another memory. Casey was home for his last leave, and the girls were complaining about his music. He liked Christian music and was listening to one of his favorite songs, one that the girls, who were into punk rock and grunge music, couldn't stand.

Not realizing how tightly wound up and worried about him I already was, I snapped at the girls, "Well, maybe Casey will be killed in Iraq and you won't have to listen to his music anymore." What a mean and hateful thing to say. I was instantly shocked and full of regret about the hurt I caused them with this thoughtless remark.

When he was home for Christmas in 2003, preparing to leave for Iraq, something was different about Casey. Even though I had only a little part-time job at the time and money was tighter than usual, I was busily trying to make this the best Christmas ever, because we knew Casey was most likely not going to be home next year. In an even bigger way than before, I could sense that Casey was not fully present with us. There was a resigned maturity about him that was almost hard to witness.

We did all of the old Sheehan family Christmas traditions for the last time. Christmas 2003 was a good Christmas with mass, stockings, presents, food, and togetherness. Auntie came up to spend the last Christmas with Casey, and on Christmas Day we did another traditional Sheehan family holiday activity.

After the kids grew up and didn't really want to stay home all day and play with their new toys, we started a new tradition of going to the movies. There is always a Christmas blockbuster to watch: 2003 was the year of *The Lord of the Rings: Return of the King.* Casey and I especially looked forward to seeing this last movie in a series that we both were really into.

Casey sat next to me in the movie theater and I could not stop hugging him or touching him or asking him if he wanted anything else. We had a wonderful time at the show. Between friends and family we took up an entire row. At one point, Janey and I were heading to the bathroom when she accidentally spilled a soda on the man in front of us and slipped on the drink, landing in the lap of another stranger. It was so funny, it is a good thing it was such a long movie, because it took us a while to recover from that one.

The last movie Casey and I saw together was *Peter Pan.* It was a live-action, very magical retelling of the classic tale. Casey and I always went to movies together. He was a theater major and we both loved the movies. The theater was so crowded that day that I dropped him off and went to park the car. When I got inside the theater, Casey was sitting in the front section with a bunch of kids. Casey and I were the only adults there without young children. At one point, one of the Darling children called one of the Indians a "savage," and a boy, much like the little man Casey had been at that age, called out, "Ha, ha, Daddy, he said 'savage' but he meant 'sausage,' huh?" Casey and I cracked up at that—I can still hear his laughter.

The day that Casey left to go back to Fort Hood after Christmas was the third saddest day of my life, after his death and burial. I had recently taken a part-time job as a bookkeeper for the restaurant where my daughter Janey worked. I wasn't making much money, but it was better than nothing. I had to go to work that morning, so Pat was going to take Casey to the airport. Before I went to work, I sat on the couch with Casey, holding him and crying. I had to wear sunglasses all day because I could not stop crying. Luckily I worked in the back office of the restaurant, so not many people noticed my emotional state.

During my shift, Casey called me from a layover in Phoenix—just to say hi and tell me that he had met another guy from the First Cav who was going to give him a ride from the airport to Fort Hood, so he wouldn't need the rental car that I had arranged for him. Then he called me again later that night when he arrived at Fort Hood.

Between the time that Casey got back to Fort Hood and left for Iraq we were in constant communication. The night before he was deployed he called and we talked for a long time. I couldn't stop crying then, either. In fact he wrote in a journal he started the next day, "Mom can't stop crying."

Casey had intended this journal to be a record of his time in

Iraq, but there was only one entry in it. Why? We don't know why he wrote only once. We can't ask him. The only entry he made was about his trip from Texas to Iraq. I am torn between wanting to know about the last few days of his life and being glad that I don't. It is so hard.

That night was the last time we really talked. I told him how proud I was of him and always had been. I thanked him for always being such a good son who never gave his dad or me any problems. I begged him and begged him to please be careful. "Please, Casey, don't take any unnecessary risks. Please come home safely!" He promised he would. He told me that his sergeant, Sergeant Spears, who was his battle buddy, had also promised me that he would bring Casey home alive. He wasn't scared, he said, he was just sorry that he was going to miss seeing *Spiderman 2,* which practically killed me when it came out the month after his death.

Casey and Sergeant Spears broke their promises to me.

Tears are pouring down my face uncontrollably while I am writing this. People who told me that only "time" could make things better were full of shit. Time does not make things better. Nothing can.

That night, Pat and I were sitting in front of the television eating our filet and watching CNN. All of a sudden, in midbite of the last meal I would ever truly enjoy, a burning humvee appeared on the screen. The voice-over said that eight soldiers had been killed in Baghdad in combat that day.

I spit out my food and said, "One of them was Casey."

This is the exact moment when Pat and I began to part ways. He started screaming at me, "It's not Casey. You don't even know where he is. He has only been there for a few days. Odds are it can't be Casey." He calmed down and said, "Look, Cindy, there are a hundred and thirty thousand soldiers there in Iraq. Odds are extremely low that one of those soldiers was Casey. He is a humvee mechanic—why would he be killed in combat?"

"Are you trying to convince me, or yourself?" I replied.

I immediately went to the computer and started to search the Internet to see if there was any news. My sister, Dede, was online and we started to instant message each other. I shared my worry with her. She tried to tell me that Casey was surrounded by a "pink bubble" and nothing could happen to him. Still my fears were not allayed. I went through the rest of the evening in a cloud of worry.

I'd realized early in Casey's deployment that the news was going to wear us out before Casey returned home. I remember Janey calling me at work one day on my cell phone and saying, "Mom, where is Casey? I just heard that a soldier was killed in Iraq." I reassured her that he was still in Kuwait, but I thought, *How is our family going to survive a year of this?*

When *The Simpsons* came on at 8 P.M., I was beginning to relax a little. I was starting to think that if I hadn't heard by then, that we'd dodged the bullet this time. I worried for the other moms.

Casey's favorite show was *The Simpsons,* as it was mine. I

would buy him the compilations every year for Christmas, and in fact, I had given him one for Christmas just a few months earlier. Ironically, that night, the episode was about Comic Book Man and Mrs. Krabapple going to a *Star Trek* convention together. Casey was a huge *Star Trek* fan. He loved every stage of the series, from the original with William Shatner to all of the subsequent incarnations. We attended a few of the conventions together and he was in heaven! On my desk at home I have a picture of Casey posing with the actor who played Q on the *Next Generation.* (I recently saw that same episode of *The Simpsons* again in a hotel room in Seattle where I was staying for a speaking engagement. I could hardly bear the pain. Grief, the "gift" that keeps on giving!) Anyway, that night I was wondering if Casey could watch it from Iraq because I knew he would enjoy it. I did not know then that he had been dead for hours.

Andy was over visiting, and after the show he went back to his own apartment. I asked our two Shih Tzu dogs, Buster and Chewy, if they wanted to go for a walk. Of course they did. So I got their leashes on them and we headed out for our usual nightly walk. Casey had a picture of these two "boys," as we called them, hanging in his room at Fort Hood. He loved animals and children.

As soon as I left the house on that warm and lovely April night, I started crying again. I knew that I could not survive an entire year with this constant worry and fear. I was planning on checking the nearby airbase to see if they had a support group for mothers with sons in combat zones. Then another horrible thought struck me. What if Casey was wounded and not dead? How could I get to him? I was a wreck all through our walk.

Buster and Chewy and I were just getting to the corner of our street when I saw that Carly had driven up—she must have gotten off work early! I was eager to talk to her some more. Seeing her there lifted my spirits a little.

I walked up to our house and as soon as I rounded the corner of the garage I could see into the living room, and even though Carly and Pat were standing there, the only thing I could see were three of the Army's Angels of Death standing in the middle of my living room.

I started to scream "No!" before I even got into the house. I let go of the dogs' leashes and I don't recall what they did. They probably ran excitedly to welcome our "visitors," as they usually do.

I staggered into the house and fell on the floor right next to the door, screaming and screaming. I can't remember how long I was screaming in what can only be described as agony when someone, I think it was Carly, pulled me up. Now I remember Pat and Carly's faces. Carly was actually standing right by the door, too, because she had just walked in the house about twenty seconds before I did. She was holding her purse with a look of horror on her face.

Pat was over by the couch holding a pair of pants in "mid-fold." His mouth was open and he had just started to cry when I came in.

I stood up and looked at the three men who I hated and who I wanted to beat and kick. Pat said, "Cindy, come over here. They need some information so they can leave."

I said, "Fuck them."

"No, Cindy, come over here and sit down," Pat said with an eerie calmness. In shock, I obeyed.

The one man said to me, "At eighteen hundred and fifty-four hours, Army Specialist Casey Sheehan was killed in action in—"

I interrupted him: "Can you please tell me in normal time, what time my son died?" He told me 6:54 P.M. Iraq time and 7:54 A.M. California time. My sweet boy had been dead all day! Carly said, "No wonder you felt good today, Mom. Casey was with you all day."

Then the man, who I never saw again, asked me for my Social Security number. "What? You just told me my son is dead and you need my Social Security number? Why?" I still don't know why. I don't know if I heard or cared about the answer.

Pat later told me that he had been sitting on the couch folding some laundry when there was a knock on the screen door. He hadn't heard the soldiers walk up and the dogs were with me, so they didn't bark.

He looked up and saw the men standing at the door. He said, "No, you can't come in. Casey can't be dead. He has only been there a week."

One of them said. "Please, sir, we have to come in."

Pat's first thought was, "Oh, poor Cindy." And the Angels

of Death dressed in Army uniforms couldn't say anything until I got home, because I was listed as Casey's "next of kin." (When soldiers are in boot camp, they have to list a "next of kin." Casey listed me. He could have put both his father and me, but he made me the full and sole beneficiary of his insurance and "next of kin." Another mystery that will never be solved, because we can't ask him.)

A few hours later some friends put me to bed and they were sitting with me. I was talking about Casey and I suddenly started worrying that maybe he had burned in that humvee that I saw on CNN. I started to scream, and the girls ran in and soothed me.

I didn't sleep for two days after Casey was killed. I didn't want to fall asleep and wake up and have to relive the news all over again. Dede and my mom got to our house sometime in the early morning, having driven all night from Los Angeles.

I was sitting on the porch swing at about 6 A.M. on April 5, and I was alone for once. Everyone else who was there, friends and family alike, had found someplace to crash and catch a few winks of sleep. I was watching our neighborhood come alive and people start to go to work. I couldn't believe that after my son was dead and my life was crushed that the fucking sun would have the nerve to come up. I was so envious of the people who were getting in their cars to go to work as if nothing had happened.

On the night of April 6, after about forty-eight hours of not sleeping and constantly crying, there were thirty or so people still at my house at about 1 A.M. My friends were starting to worry more about me because I couldn't sleep. A few of them came up to me and whispered, "Here, take this, it will help you sleep." I would take the pill, whatever it was (I never asked), and wash it down with a swallow of beer. After I don't know how many beers and pills, I finally crashed at about four that morning—then got up at six—throwing up but ready to meet a new day of grieving and visitors.

I don't know how many visitors we had in the nine days between the time we found out and the time we buried Casey—which I guess is the official signal to stop visiting a family. But we always had dozens of people at our house, and the weather was so nice most of us sat on the front lawn. We had impromptu concerts and barbecues, and there was always too much food. Someone was always running to the store for beer and ice.

A thoughtful friend brought over toilet paper and tissues; our toilets were always stopping up because our forty-year-old plumbing was not strong enough to withstand the constant use.

As in all wakes, there was plenty of laughter to mingle with the tears. We all had great memories of Casey and our times together and we were all a little irreverent, too. I wonder if there was ever a nine-day wake that had such sustained presence, laughter, and tears!

One night, there were about twenty of us still at the house and it was nearing midnight. My sister, Dede, looked up and said, "Dad is standing right over there." Now, remember, my dad had been dead for ten years at this point. Dede pointed at something and the only thing all of us could see was the wall. Then she said, "Wow, Casey is standing right over there." So she got up and was feeling the place where she said Casey was standing.

A few people, including Carly, joined her and Carly said, "Mom, come here and feel this, it really is Casey." I went over and felt the obvious warmth and love in the space in the middle of our circled friends. Dede gasped and said, "Cindy, he just kissed your cheek." I collapsed on the floor in tears and Carly joined me, facing me. She looked up in surprise and I felt my son kiss me on my lips. His kiss was so warm and filled with so much love that it could not be an earthly love. His love came from a deep universal place now.

I said, "Oh, my God, he just kissed me on the lips!" and put my hand on my mouth to trap the warmth there. Carly said, "I know, Mom, he reached over me to kiss you."

The time between the day that we all went to pick him up at the airport in his cardboard box to the moment when we said our final good-byes to him and lowered him in the grave is like a movie to me. I felt like I was watching any movie I had ever seen about a hero—and I was starring in it. None of it felt real, which is probably a good thing, because I don't know how one would get through something like that if it were real.

It was so sad to go to the airport in San Francisco in a limo to pick up Casey. We were all crying, thinking about the joyous times when he had returned home to visit since he joined the

Army. I can never go to an airport anywhere in the world and not be forced to recall picking my son up the way we had to. And I am in a lot of airports every week.

The day after we picked Casey up from the airport was the viewing day. Steve, the mortician, called after he got Casey's packing crate open and told us he had died from a gunshot wound to the back of the head, but otherwise he looked as if he were "sleeping." This was the first indication that we had of how Casey died. The Army wouldn't tell us. We didn't know until a year after he died that he was alive when he got to the post and a medic had to try to hold his brains in while the docs tried to save his life. His brains were too scrambled, and he would have been horribly compromised if he had lived. I found out much later that a bullet had somehow gotten under his helmet and had ricocheted back there because it was trapped by the Kevlar "protection."

I have received so many conflicting reports about what happened to Casey on 04/04/04. From the official Army report to stories from his buddies on the scene to embedded reporters' accounts, it is all very confusing. (The Department of Defense website says that the incident is still "under investigation.")

This is the truth from what I can piece together: 6:00 P.M., Baghdad time, the First Cavalry took over control of Forward Operating Base War Eagle, in Sadr City, from the First Armored Division. By 6:54 P.M., Casey was dead.

This is what I heard from Casey's buddies, other vets of this war and other wars, and the reporters who were there: Right after the base changed command, a call came through to the post that a group of soldiers who were out on patrol in this teeming slum of Baghdad had been ambushed and they were taking heavy casualties. Casey's chief was told to put together a "quick response force" to go and rescue the soldiers who were pinned down by the insurgents. Casey's chief and other soldiers who were not there, but who came to Casey's funeral, told us that Casey volunteered. Other soldiers from Vietnam and Iraq tell me that this is the way 99 percent of soldiers volunteer: The superior points at each soldier and says, "You, you, you, and you: you volunteer." I have been told that this is so if the unthinkable happens to the soldier and he is killed, the family can be told that he "died a hero." As though this is supposed to be some kind of comfort or solace to the mother of the dead soldier. Casey's chief said that he told Casey that he didn't have to go but Casey said, "Where my chief goes, I go."

I have further reason to doubt Casey's chief's account because he also told us that Casey died in his arms on the battlefield, when I have heard from one of the doctors and a medic who worked on Casey that he was still breathing when he got to the med-center.

A few soldiers said that Casey's group was ambushed in a dark alley on the way to the rescue mission. Shots rang out, "Man down" was heard, and that's about all I know.

My boy's death certificate reads: "KIA. Hostile Fire. Gunshot wound to head."

I could never understand why Pat was so relieved that we

could view Casey. I didn't want my last memory of him to be of him lying in a coffin. I guess it is a Catholic thing, but I have always thought that viewings are kind of barbaric. Being able to be with Casey gave Pat and Andy and other members of our family great comfort, though. The girls and I each separately went to see him very briefly, but I couldn't look at him for long, or even get within about five feet of the coffin.

When Casey was born, he had a squished face from coming out of the birth canal, and we called him Edward G. Robinson for a while, until his face perked up. God help me, when he was in his coffin and with his face muscles slack, he looked like Edward G. all over again, and he could have been sleeping in his bassinet.

At his funeral, I was handed some more "man scout" badges by a general who was about a foot shorter than I am, and at the burial the same general handed me a folded flag. We buried Casey in his dress greens, and I wonder why. Why did I allow my son to be buried as a soldier and not as a human being?

Why did we have a twenty-one-gun salute? What the hell was that all about anyway? Was it re-creating the battle where he was killed? Does anyone know why they put shotgun shells in the flag before they fold it up? Why didn't I put one of Casey's sweat suits on him and his ever-present baseball cap instead of his greens? Everyone told me at the time that "Casey would want it that way." Like a good scout, I went along with all the militaristic rigmarole. Not anymore.

Heroes are not created on battlefields. They are created in

homes, in towns large and small, by loving families who want only the best for their children.

Victims and martyrs are created by the war machine that only wants our heroes for profit.

I wish I'd known that before Casey was killed—but I also wish that I didn't have to know it now.

Chapter 5

A Nation Rocked to Sleep and a Mom Rudely Awakened

*"If we the people let them continue,
another mother will weep."*
—CARLY SHEEHAN, APRIL 2004

ONE LOVELY APRIL DAY (ALL THE DAYS FROM CASEY'S death until about Thanksgiving were lovely), my journal says that it was April 27, I was sitting on the couch—my famous couch—crying. I missed Casey so much. I never knew such longing existed in the universe. I felt like a piece of rotted meat surrounded by flies and ugliness. I felt wrung out and dehydrated by the tears that wouldn't stop. I remember being always amazed at the amount of fluid that a body can produce. Besides the crying and going through the motions of life, I was otherwise paralyzed by my pain and longing.

I was feeling that dying would be preferable to the pain. Every night I had to restrain myself from taking my entire bottle of sleeping pills instead of just one. The only things that stopped me from the very appealing idea of falling asleep and never waking up again were Carly, Andy, and Janey. How could I put them through another death? In my case, committing suicide would have been the ultimate act of selfishness.

But the pain was so intense! I thought I'd had my heart broken in the past by old boyfriends, or former friends who had stabbed me in the back by not acting very friendly, but I had never truly had my heart broken until Casey died. The pain of a broken heart is so intense because it is physical and emotional. At that point in my life, the loss of hope was also completely devastating. Going through the motions of life is nothing like actually living.

For about a month after Casey was killed, we were getting about eighty to a hundred pieces of mail a day. Some were just addressed to: Spc. Casey Sheehan's family, Vacaville, California, and they still got to us. Some were sent to Fort Hood and forwarded to us, and some were even sent to St. Mary's, where Casey's funeral mass was held.

In these cards and letters, our family and Casey were lauded for our "sacrifice" for Freedom and Democracy (always capitalized). We received letters from George Bush and Donald Rumsfeld that were signed by machines.

We received a particularly moving letter from "Freedom

Fries" Republican congressman Walter Jones of North Carolina, who included the following quote:

> He stands in the unbroken line of patriots who have dared to die. That freedom may live, and grow, and increase its blessings. Freedom lives, and through it, he lives—In a way that humbles the undertakings of most men.
>
> *Franklin D. Roosevelt*

When I read this letter from Representative Jones, I laid my head on Pat's lap and wept. I immediately sent a letter of gratitude to Walter Jones, and later we were to become allies in peace when he changed his mind about the war and asked for my forgiveness for voting to give George Bush the authority to invade Iraq. On that day, I sobbed for all the mothers who have had their children killed for greed.

On this twenty-seventh day of April, though, about three weeks after Casey was killed, I was reading another poem that a well-meaning but misguided American had sent me, saying how wonderful it was that Casey died to keep us safe, free, and blah, blah, blah.

Well, I didn't believe that line of bullshit before Casey was killed, and I certainly didn't believe it after he was killed. Casey didn't die to keep me or anyone freer . . . he died to feed and enrich the war machine.

Gen. Smedley D. Butler, who was the most decorated

Marine of his time, says in his courageous and prescient book, *War Is a Racket,* written after World War I:

> War is a racket. It always has been.
>
> It is possibly the oldest, easily the most profitable, surely the most vicious. It is the only one international in scope. It is the only one in which the profits are reckoned in dollars and the losses in lives.
>
> A racket is best described, I believe, as something that is not what it seems to the majority of the people. Only a small "inside" group knows what it is about. It is conducted for the benefit of the very few, at the expense of the very many. Out of war a few people make huge fortunes.

Does anyone remember World War I? The war to end all wars? When the use of chemical weapons and the targeting of civilians were perfected? When dissent was unpatriotic and the waving of the American flag was frenetic?

Anyone who has children now, or who is even contemplating maybe having children some day, should be required to read *War Is a Racket* before conception.

In my apathetic, ignorant, materialistic, and TV-logged brain, I was dimly aware that war was big business. But war touched me in only a very peripheral way until it came crashing down around my entire being on April 4, 2004.

Through a grief- and pain-drenched heart, I started to research the Iraq war, the Afghanistan war, the war machine, all war. I ran across General Butler's short but powerful book. If I had read it earlier in my existence, I am sure Casey would still be alive.

I am now convinced that Casey died to put food on the war machine's table. Casey's flesh and blood sends the war machine's children to exclusive private schools. Casey was murdered by the war machine. I didn't feel safer for his sacrifice. I felt like I was put in a prison of grief and unending pain.

Carly walked up to me one day when I was at my lowest, the ever-present snot running out of my nose, and the tears streaming from my eyes, and she said, "Mom, do you want to hear a poem I wrote?"

Even through my heartache, I was and am still a proud mom of three living children, so I said, "Of course, honey!" I was honored; Carly is a great poet.

Little did I know on that April day back in 2004, but Carly's poem was about to rock my world as much as Casey's death. At that moment in time, I was transformed. And the transformation was not a minor event for me: my shape shifted. I became a shape-shifter on that day.

I was transformed from an ordinary human being into a crusader.

I was transformed from a private mother into a public peace mom.

I was transformed from a shy and horrible public speaker into a brave and powerful orator.

I was transformed from a nonwriter into an able author on fire for the truth.

I was transformed from a peaceful person into a total pacifist.

I was transformed from an apathetic American into a soon-to-be "superactivist" for peace.

So, through my pain-soaked existence, I listened to the inspired words of my daughter (and her brother Casey, I am convinced), and my life was not only transformed, it was saved.

In a voice quivering with sorrow, Carly read these words to me:

Have you ever heard the sound of a mother screaming
  for her son?
The torrential rains of a mother's weeping will never
  be done.
They call him a hero, you should be glad that he's
  one, but,
Have you ever heard the sound of a mother screaming
  for her son.

Have you ever heard the sound of a father holding
  back his cries?

Cindy Sheehan

60

They say he must be brave because his boy died for
  another man's lies.
The only thing he allows himself are long, deep sighs.
Have you ever heard the sound of a father holding
  back his cries.

Have you ever heard the sound of taps played at your
  brother's grave?
They say he died so the flag will continue to wave.
But I believe he died because they had oil to save.
Have you ever heard the sound of taps played at your
  brother's grave?

Have you ever heard the sound of a nation being
  rocked to sleep?
Our leaders want to keep you numb, so the pain
  won't be so deep.
But if we the people let them continue, another
  mother will weep.
Have you ever heard the sound of a nation being
  rocked to sleep?

I was stunned. I sat on my couch stunned by the depth, honesty, pain, and relevance of this poem. When Carly told me she
wrote it in "about ten minutes," I knew that Casey must have
been sitting next to her and whispering in her ear—an angelic

collaboration. Using Carly's innate brilliance and Casey's divine knowledge, they created the one thing that would get me off my apathetic ass and onto the path that I came to earth to follow.

I say Carly's poem saved my life because she gave me a reason for living.

I had known that Casey was killed in an illegal and immoral war based on the imaginations of the president and his nefarious band of neocons, but I hadn't done anything with my knowledge.

I got the wake-up call at 9 P.M. on the evening of April 4, and knowing how horrible that wake-up call was, how could I just lie on the couch and wallow in my own pain when there were millions of people still in harm's way?

I knew at that minute that I would have to do something to wake this nation from a slumber that was allowing our leaders to kill innocent people. A slumber that wouldn't allow the images from Iraq or the flag-draped coffins to be shown on the news.

I knew the task was going to be difficult and uphill. I never imagined how difficult, or how steep the hill was, or how much more my new mission was going to cost me.

I have often been asked by the media if I would step out onto this path again if I knew how much my actions were going to cost me.

The answer is yes.

There was and still is too much at stake not to put myself into the struggle with both feet and with 100 percent of my resources—monetary, physical, and emotional. I want my children and their unborn children to live in a world of peace and plenty, where everyone feels safe and loved. I want them to have the world that I didn't have the courage or the wisdom to give Casey. I want to be able to look in their eyes and say, "Grandma did everything she could to give you a better life."

I was recently at a dinner with "Hanoi" Jane Fonda—we always joke about being Hanoi Jane and Baghdad Cindy, because we know how hypocritical those epithets are. A man sitting next to Jane at this dinner told her that she had saved his life by her actions in North Vietnam during that nightmare war. Because of her efforts, the traitorous leadership of our country at that time started to pull back to avoid the horrible PR the war machine was already getting by then.

If one person comes to me in thirty years and tells me that I saved his or her life, then every insult hurled at me, every death threat I have received, every name I have been called, and the death of what being Cindy Sheehan and the Sheehan family means, will have been worth it.

Saving lives is a sacred thing. Jesus said: "Sometimes you have to lose your life to save it."

My life was saved by my daughter. Now what could I do to save others?

Carly's poem has been the catalyst for my activism and for change around the world. She inspired me and so many others directly, and she has inspired millions of others through her mom's work.

Carly is as big a hero as Casey.

All my children are heroes, because they have had to sacrifice the death of our family and they hold their heads high and continue to live value-centered lives.

That is also sacred.

Chapter 6

Close Encounters of the Bush Kind

"Mom, I can't imagine how you feel."
—GEORGE BUSH, JUNE 18, 2004

AS I HAVE WRITTEN BEFORE, WHEN GEORGE BUSH WAS selected by the Supreme Court at the end of 2000, I was devastated. I couldn't believe that this miscreant of a Texas governor who set that state back decades in terms of health care, education, the environment, capital punishment, etc., was going to be the leader of the free world.

I couldn't believe that the draft-dodging, dry-drunk, drug-abusing, C- student with a below-average intellect was about to be sworn in as my president. . . .

At that time I didn't know about Karl Rove or the neocons, or the Project for the New American Century.

I didn't know that in 1999, George Bush had told Mickey Herskowitz, a respected journalist and longtime Bush family friend who interviewed Bush when he was just a candidate for president: "One of the keys to being seen as a great leader is to be seen as a commander in chief. My father had all this political capital built up when he drove the Iraqis out of Kuwait and he wasted it. If I have a chance to invade . . . if I had that much capital, I'm not going to waste it. I'm going to get everything passed that I want to get passed and I'm going to have a successful presidency." It looks like George Bush was ready to lead this country into an avoidable war even before he became president.

I had never heard of Karl Rove even during Bush's ill-fated first campaign. I started hearing about him during the second campaign, after Casey was already dead and I was campaigning against George Bush during the 2004 presidential election debacle.

I found out that Rove had been into dirty politics for years in Texas and then carried them to Washington, D.C., with his subpar candidate, who became an unconstitutional and illegitimate president. Karl Rove is implicated in everything from breaking into the offices of candidates to outing CIA agent Valerie Plame, in retribution after her husband, former acting ambassador to Iraq Joseph Wilson, dared tell the truth about the Niger connection in the yellow-cake uranium lie.

I never imagined in my wildest dreams that I would be connected to Karl Rove and George Bush.

In the year 2000 I had never even heard the term *neoconservative,* shortened to *neocon.* I didn't know what such people as Richard Perle, Paul Wolfowitz (a major architect of the Iraq

War), Douglas Feith, Dick Cheney, Donald Rumsfeld, and William Kristol had been plotting for at least three decades. I didn't know that in 1997 the above people and many others had started the Project for the New American Century (PNAC).

Here's what the organization's own website says about them:

> The Project for the New American Century is a non-profit educational organization dedicated to a few fundamental propositions: that American leadership is good both for America and for the world; and that such leadership requires military strength, diplomatic energy, and commitment to moral principle.

> The Project for the New American Century intends, through issue briefs, research papers, advocacy journalism, conferences, and seminars, to explain what American world leadership entails. It will also strive to rally support for a vigorous and principled policy of American international involvement and to stimulate useful public debate on foreign and defense policy and America's role in the world.

Obviously, the PNAC is a plan for American empire and hegemony of the world, to essentially foist this "leadership" anywhere in the world. All of these forces converged in 2000, when many neocons attained prominent positions in the new

Bush administration. Combined with the new president's resolve to invade Iraq and to be seen as a strong "commander in chief," Casey, my family, and the world were doomed.

George Bush's first secretary of the Treasury, Paul O'Neill (later fired for insubordination), has said many times in interviews and in Ron Suskind's book *The Price of Loyalty* that invading Iraq was on the minds of many in the administration at the first cabinet meeting in January of 2001, nine months before September 11.

In July 2002, as recorded in the Downing Street Memo, a recent visitor to the United States told England's prime minister, Tony Blair, that the invasion of Iraq was now a "foregone" conclusion and the intelligence to justify the invasion needed to be "fixed around the policy" of invading Iraq.

We now know that in early February 2003, Colin Powell gave a performance based on "hoax" intelligence (according to Powell's chief aide, Larry Wilkerson) to the U.N. We also now know that in late January of 2003, Blair and Bush met in the Oval Office and agreed that if they didn't get a second resolution from the U.N., they would invade Iraq anyway. And wouldn't it be nice if Saddam attacked one of our planes that we were flying over Iraq to provoke an attack?

Well, we also all know now that Saddam did not have weapons of mass destruction or any connection to al Qaeda or 9/11.

On March 19, 2003, George Bush shocked and awed the world with his preemptive, illegal, and immoral invasion of Iraq.

I remember that night, sitting on the same couch where I last held Casey, watching the bombs drop on Baghdad and wondering where the hell reason had gone.

I sat on my couch not knowing any of the things that I have just written about but knowing in my gut that George, Condi, Dick, Colin, and Don were lying through their collective asses and selling a war to the public based on fear of "terrorism."

I sat on my couch crying tears of anguish for the Iraqi people and for our soldiers—and their families—who were put in harm's way on behalf of the desperadoes of disaster. I was grateful, for the moment, that Casey was not there. However, he was scheduled to be deployed in April of 2003. What a joyous day it was when we found out that the First Cav had been given a one-year reprieve from going. I was hoping against hope and everything I knew that this invasion was going to be the "cakewalk" that Dick Cheney said it was going to be.

I didn't do anything about my anguish and anger until the war came home to roost for me on April 4, 2004.

After Casey was killed in Iraq, I walked through my days in a state of pain that was and still is both physical and emotional.

My tears were ever present . . . or not too far from the surface.

May is one of the nicest months in California—particularly in the Sacramento Valley, where it can get fried-egg-on-the-sidewalk hot during the summer. May is the gorgeous spring transition between the frosty and rainy valley winters and the hot summers.

Casey was born in May.

May is the month of Mother's Day.

Pat was born in May.

We have a long weekend in May.

The Sheehan family used to barbecue and rejoice in spring every Memorial Day . . . and we would usually combine the " 'cues" with a birthday party for Casey, who was born on May 29. We did this from his first birthday to his twenty-first birthday, right before he went into the Army.

On Casey's birthday in 2004, the annual Fiesta Day parade in Vacaville was dedicated to heroes, and a company in town designed their entire entry to honor Casey and another man who had lived in Vacaville for a short time and who was also killed in the war. And Casey's Boy Scout troop had instituted the Casey Austin Sheehan Memorial Award, which they gave to the winner that same day at the cemetery.

After those two events, we went to a friend's house and had a huge "birthday" party for Casey. My stomach ached all day. I know it was aching for Casey. I know it was aching because I couldn't buy him presents and send them to him in Iraq. I know it was aching because I had to try to act so damn happy around my friends, who were already starting to worry about me.

I wrote this in my journal on May 29, 2004:

Dear Casey,

Happy Birthday my sweet son!

25 years ago today you came into our lives.

As soon as your head came out of me, you started screaming.

I don't think you wanted to come back! You made a bargain with God that you'd come back to earth as long as you didn't have to stay too long.

Did you like the parade, the service at your park and your party?

Everything was so nice for you!

I hope when I die, I will be ½ as loved as you. I already wish I was as brave as you! This life is so hard to face without you, honey.

I love you so much and I miss you so much. I have a very bad tummy ache. This has been a long busy week. I'm extremely exhausted—it's hard enough grieving you without having so much stuff to do.

Love you so much!

Mom

If I heard "Casey wouldn't want you to be so sad" one more time, I was afraid I was going to start screaming and not stop until every blood vessel in my head and heart exploded.

Only people who have never buried a child say that.

Another platitude is "He's in a better place." Well, yes, Heaven is better than a war zone . . . but how about home with his mother? I know people just don't know what to say, so they resort to clichés. I think if one doesn't have anything comforting to say (and there isn't really anything comforting to say!), then it's better not to say anything.

Another thing many people told me after Casey was killed, and I think they said this to assuage their own consciences, was "Casey died doing what he loved doing."

Oh, really. Casey joined the Army because his recruiter, whose name I have forgotten but whom I call "Sgt. Big Fat Liar," told him he could be a chaplain's assistant and never see combat even if "there is a war." Casey didn't want to be a humvee mechanic and he certainly didn't want to die in a god-forsaken land thousands of miles from home, fighting a people who only wanted him out of their country. I hope these people who thought Casey wanted to have his brains mangled and his life snuffed out for a lie have had a change of heart. If not, they should go to Iraq and do the job that they say Casey wanted to do and carry a gun and wear the uniform of the war profiteers.

A grieving mother needs hugs, lots and lots of hugs; tissues, lots and lots of tissues; water, lots and lots of water. That's what a grieving mom needs. Not meaningless and hurtful expressions that I now suspect have been meaningless and hurtful throughout the years. I hope I have never hurt any grieving soul by saying any of these things.

I used to love May. May is now the month of my bottomless mourning.

I was urged by Pat and so many of our friends to return to

work as soon as possible to "take my mind off of things." I didn't want to go back to work, and I certainly had a sneaking suspicion that turned out to be confirmed that I would never be able to "take my mind off" Casey being killed.

I had just started a new job for the County of Napa in Health and Human Services a few weeks before Casey was killed. Our family was thrilled, because after almost two years of no benefits and spotty employment for me, it looked as if we were going to get on a more stable financial footing. The job paid well, had awesome benefits including a pension, and offered great opportunity for advancement.

I went back to work three weeks after Casey was killed. I cried all the way to work. I was alone for the first time for any length of time. Even though the people I worked for and with were very flexible and understanding, no one knew me, and I think they were a little afraid of my grief. No one knew what to say to me. My supervisor's son was over in Iraq and she couldn't look at me without having to face her worst fears.

It was the most uncomfortable feeling to be grieving in my own little office, in a building filled with strangers, isolated from my family and having nothing to think about but Casey and people who wanted Medi-Cal—and I really couldn't think or care about them. I walked around with stomachaches and a feeling like my heart was going to pound its way out of my chest.

On the drive home from work on that first day back, I experienced the first in a long series of panic attacks. I started screaming in the traffic of I-80 and I couldn't stop. I thought I was going to break some blood vessels in my brain or that my heart would explode like the IEDs that were taking the lives of our children and the children of Iraq. I pulled off the highway and waited for the panic attack and the screaming to stop. I wonder how someone could scream like that without doing permanent damage to her body or even killing herself.

I called my doctor from my cell phone and went straight to her office. She put me on half days after scolding me about going back to work so soon after Casey was killed. Pat was with me and was very adamant about me staying at work—he felt it was best for me to work. I look back on those days and realize that I was not fit for work—I was barely fit to get out of bed. Just typing this and recalling those days, I start to feel a wee bit panicky. It was horrible.

One day when I was at work, Pat called and told me that we were invited to go and have a "sit down" with the president at Fort Lewis, Washington. I said, "What president?"

And he said, "The president of the United States!"

That was on a Tuesday. By Thursday morning, our entire family was flying via Alaska Airlines to Seattle, Washington.

This trip was the first time the five of us were going to be alone together as a family since Casey had been killed. We tried to be "normal." Pat and I tried not to fight. We tried, but it didn't quite work.

We checked in at Terminal 2 at the Sacramento airport. We were going up the escalator to security when we heard a very calm and kind-sounding lady telling us over the loudspeaker: "Please step forward after getting off of the escalator." For some reason this tickled all of us. We wondered how we had managed to effectively and safely use escalators before then. It was almost as if we had some instinctive urge to always step forward off escalators before. Is this stepping-forward-off-escalators skill something humans are born with? Or is it something we have to learn? We cracked ourselves up taking a few steps then waiting for the kind lady to tell us what to do. But we were confused from that point on, because there were no further instructions from her.

When we got to the Seattle airport, we were met by two sergeants from Fort Lewis. They took us to our hotel near the post, and after we checked in, we rented a car and went back to Seattle to do some sightseeing.

We had a semiwonderful time and we laughed a lot and felt Casey's presence most strongly when we were laughing.

After twenty-four years of being a family, we knew pretty much how road trips would go. Casey would get carsick and I would have to change places with him. Andy would get goofy and we would have to stop about every half hour so he could pee. Janey would put on headphones and listen to music and Carly would read—all of this while Pat was crabby—and I would try to make the best of everything until Pat's crabbiness got to me and I became crabby, too.

Well, this road trip was different because Casey wasn't there to get carsick and Carly and Janey didn't use the time to withdraw. Andy still was goofy and had to pee a lot—which is always fine with me because I have to go a lot, too.

Those two days we were in Seattle were rare days for them. The temperature was 85 degrees and the citizens of Seattle were sweating and complaining about how hot it was. They all were red as lobsters and looked so miserable. We had just come from 100-degree weather in Vacaville, so we were very comfortable and felt fresh and cool.

I look back on the pictures of that day—Pat and I together, the kids in front of the fountain near the Space Needle—we look like a normal, happy family. But at that time nothing could have been further from the truth. We would go on two more trips together as a family, and by the second one Pat and I had almost reached the point of no return, and by the third one, we had passed that point. I will write more about the death of our family in a later chapter, but in Seattle, we were still doing okay.

The night before we went to meet George Bush, we went to sleep early because we had to get up early. We were supposed to be at the bus by 6:15 A.M. to make the trip to Fort Lewis. We got a six-pack of Heineken and we each enjoyed a beer before the girls went to their room and Andy went to his room.

We were a little late getting to the bus the next morning because at first we couldn't get Andy up—either by phone or by knocking on his door. When we boarded the bus we were greeted by approximately sixty people, making up fourteen or fifteen families like ours. All the others had the same sad look around their eyes. There was no jocularity or singing on this bus.

I met a young woman whose husband had been blown to vapor and they'd recovered nothing of him to bury. His mom and dad were also on the bus. They were so hurt and fragile.

But sitting right in front of me was another woman whom I have grown to dislike very strongly. I soon found out that she was the stepmother of a soldier who was killed, but she introduced herself and her husband as the parents of "Ed." She then pointed out another woman who she said was Ed's "sort of foster mother"—who I found out later was Ed's real mother. The first woman was his stepmother, who didn't have a very good relationship with Ed before he was killed. But ever since he was killed, she has been a tireless supporter of the war and the president. She is so "brave and valiant" to keep her chin up after her stepson was killed.

This stepmother and her husband became active participants in one of the most bizarre protests in history: The "Cindy doesn't speak for me" tour. I can't believe that these people's views, beliefs, and intellect are so wee that they can't even have a "We speak for ourselves" tour. Ed's real mother, who is very antiwar and anti-Bush, is in my organization and her heart aches every time this woman claims Ed as her own and exploits his name and sacrifice to prop up the president and his misguided war.

We arrived at Fort Lewis about forty-five minutes after we left the hotel. Then we had to stand in the parking lot of the post hospital, where the meetings were to occur, for another hour because they weren't ready to let us in yet. I was beginning to feel the Washington State "heat wave" more acutely as we stood on asphalt without shade or water.

This interlude, though, is when I found out that my soon to be new friend was Ed's mother, not his "sort of foster mother." I found out that she was even more deeply opposed to George Bush and the war than I was at the time. Her son was KIA back in 2003, so she'd had a little more time to ponder the reasons and lies. She even had a letter that she wanted to give George, accusing him of lying and taking our country to war for oil. *Damn it,* I thought to myself, *I wish I had thought of that!*

My new friend "Donna" requested, and received, a meeting with George Bush that was separate from the one with her flag-waving, red-white-and-blue-wearing ex-husband and his wife. She gave the letter to one of the president's aides and waited in a room by herself until George had met with all of the other families. I wish to recount her meeting before I recount ours. Then maybe, dear reader, you won't be so horrified by our little "tea party" with George.

Donna was waiting in her little curtained-off area for the president to appear. When he did, he strode right up to her and put his face an inch from hers—there they stood, nose to nose, and Donna, God bless her, did not back off. He sneered at her and said in his most intimidating (he thinks) voice, "I'm George W. Bush, I am president of the United States, and I hear you have something to say to me."

Donna looked him squarely in the eye and said, "You bet I do."

She then went on to outline her grievances against him, asking the question that I would try to ask George a year later: "Why did my son have to die?"

Donna told him that Ed had a good life and if he had lived, he would have been a productive and wonderful citizen of our society. Then Bush said the coldest thing to her that I have ever heard. After Donna got through talking about her dear boy, George, unbelievably and incredibly, said, "If your son came home from Iraq alive, how do you know he would have had a good life?"

When Donna told me that, I wondered how she didn't slap him or spit in his face. President or not, that was a rude and coldhearted and pitiless thing to say. She said she was too shocked to even say anything in reply.

Our meeting with George was disturbing, but it took us a while to realize it because we were still in too much shock at the time to process it.

We were moved from a big room in the post hospital to a little room with a couch, chair, a coffee table, and a fake potted tree. The room was a curtained-off space that was barely big enough for the five of us. I had brought five pictures of Casey, ranging from when he was a baby to when he was a big soldier man.

The smiling pictures of a cheerful and chubby-cheeked baby break my heart. Why did I let my sunny, wonderful boy join Uncle Sam's army? The pictures of Casey when he was a beautiful boy are heartbreaking, too. Then he became an awkward teenager—tall and skinny and all "asses and elbows," as I used to say to him—with braces and acne, to boot! When the braces came off and the acne cleared, he was a handsome young man.

So we were sitting in this tiny room at Fort Lewis with the pictures of Casey on the coffee table. The scene was like some tragic and smaller version of our home and our decimated family. We were nervously waiting for George Bush to appear—when in walked Arizona senator John McCain.

The events that I am about to relate were later disputed by John McCain, but I know they are the truth. Up to that point in my life, I had never even met one senator, let alone one with the stature of John McCain, and I treasured what he said to us.

The senator was very personable and he sat right down on the couch and complimented the girls on how pretty they were and on how handsome Andy was—he called us all by our first names—then he looked at the pictures of Casey and had tears in his eyes.

I asked McCain why Casey had to die, and he told me, "Well, Cindy, I am afraid it's going to be for nothing, like my buddies in Vietnam." I was stunned by his openness and honesty, but I deeply appreciated it. However, he denies having said this.

We chatted with some small talk and then he asked us if there was anything else he could do for us and I said, "Yes, you can run with Senator Kerry as his vice president." He chuckled and said, "Anything but that, Cindy. The country is too divided as it is." Senator McCain remembers this exchange. We had quite a spirited talk about this, our first meeting, when I met with him again in his Washington, D.C., office in September.

I had a lot of respect for Senator McCain, and I love what he did in the Senate to try to limit George and Dick's reign of torture. But after what the Rove team did to John McCain during the 2000 campaign when they smeared him and tried to aver that he had a black baby and demeaned his war record as a prisoner of war in Vietnam—trying to make him look as if he gave up national secrets under torture—then John McCain bends over and lets George Bush kiss him. He even campaigned for Bush in 2004. That's when I lost respect for the senator, but in June 2004, I still had a lot of regard for him. Now, with the senator's unending support for another Vietnam-style war, I fear that every shred of goodness and humanity in him has been lost.

After the senator left our little "living room," we looked at each other, and Carly said, "I wonder if he is the president's warm-up act." And Pat said, "I wonder what Casey has in store for us next."

After what seemed like hours, the curtain finally opened and in walked George. I was face-to-face with the devil, but I didn't even know how monstrous this person really was yet.

The president of the United States of America, arguably the most powerful man in the world, walked into the room wearing a blue suit that looked straight off a Wal-Mart rack. His entire tone was one of being at a tea party, and the first thing he uttered was, "So, who are we honorin' here?"

We all looked at one another in disbelief, and later, when we compared notes, we couldn't believe that the so-called leader of the so-called free world didn't even know Casey's name. And unlike the senator, he didn't know our names, because right before George entered they had us take off our name tags. I think this was to make it a better photo op, but I'm not really sure. At the very least, we couldn't believe that an aide didn't whisper, "Mr. President, this is the Sheehan family. Their son, Specialist Casey Sheehan, was killed in Iraq."

So we told him who we were and who *we* were "honorin'." We are still not sure who he honors, and I am not sure we really want to know.

I tried to get George to look at the pictures that we had brought of Casey, but he wouldn't. We tried to talk about Casey and what a valuable member of our family he was, but he didn't want to hear it. He didn't want to know anything about Casey, and I feel he didn't want to see the face of someone his lies killed. I believe George does not want to humanize his cannon fodder, or bullet sponges, as the soldiers call themselves.

At one point he approached Carly and said, "Who are you to the loved one?" (He always called Casey the "loved one.") Carly replied, "Casey was my brother."

George then said a very stupid thing, which he is famous for: "I wish I could bring your loved one back to fill the hole in your hearts."

"So do we, Mr. President," Carly agreed. At which point he

gave her what Carly says was the "dirtiest look I ever received from another human being" and said to her, "I'm sure you do." Then he dismissed Carly with a turn of his back and never spoke to her again for the rest of the meeting.

We had some presidential small talk. He wanted to know what we did for a living and was particularly interested in Andy's career as a surveyor. We took some pictures with him, and he said to the kids, "Take care of your mama, she has a very sweet soul."

Then he approached me for our infamous exchange. He took my right hand in both of his and said, "Mom"—he called me Mom—"I can't imagine losin' a loved one. Whether it is an aunt, uncle, niece, nephew, brother, sister . . ."

Before he could go through the entire litany of how Casey could be related to me without actually saying the word *son*, I stopped him and said, "Mr. President"—that's when I still called him that—"Casey was my son. I think you can imagine it—you have two daughters—try to imagine one of them being killed." I saw a brief flicker of humanity in his eyes, then it was gone. I said, "Trust me, Mr. President, you don't want to go there."

And he said, "You're right, I don't."

At least, and I think for the first time, he was honest. I was stunned at his coldhearted statement and all I could mutter was, "Well, thanks for putting me there."

George Bush stammered some things about everyone on

earth deserving "freedom and democracy" and slobbered something else about "expressing the thanks of a grateful nation." Trust me, we didn't say "You're welcome." Then as fast as he swept in, the tea party was over.

When I say George pretended to have compassion it is because everything he said did not match his eyes. Speaking to him was like speaking to someone who is disconnected from reality. It is very disconcerting to talk to people when the heart light of their eyes does not match what they are saying.

It was a very disordered event, not quite but almost as disordered as burying a child.

One of the things I asked him when we were speaking was, "Why were we invited here? We didn't vote for you in 2000 and we are certainly not going to vote for you this year!" His answer to me was, "Mom, this is not about politics." For some unknown but totally forgivable reason I believed him. That is, until the Republican National Convention, when he betrayed my trust again.

In his acceptance speech for the nomination for president, he said something like, "I meet with the families of the fallen. I feel their pain. They tell me that they are praying for me and to complete the mission in Iraq so their loved ones don't die in vain." That is what tore it for me. He told me he wasn't meeting us for political reasons, but that's exactly what it was for. The so-called commander in chief doesn't allow the showing of images of flag-draped coffins coming home from Iraq nor has he attended a single funeral.

He was trying to assure the nation that he had compassion. He was trying to tell the nation that we wanted more children killed just because Casey was dead.

Again, and again, and again, and again, he was lying. That's when I decided to become involved in the 2004 presidential campaign. Not to campaign for John Kerry, but to campaign against George Bush.

Chapter 7

The Struggle Begins

*Hard work is burying your child 46 days
before his 25th birthday.*
— Cindy Sheehan in an open letter
to George W. Bush

AS SOON AS CASEY WAS KILLED, I STARTED TO CLOSE
up on myself.

I had horrible back and neck spasms, and I discovered that a
broken heart wasn't just an expression: it was a literal pain that
hurt worse than any broken toe or finger I had ever suffered.
Women always talk about how painful childbirth is. Child
death is far more painful; it's like having a vital part of oneself
amputated without anesthesia. And at the end of the day, you
don't have a cute little miracle of a human being to nurse and
nuzzle with, you have a sterile burial plot that, no matter how
nice the location is and how sweetly the wind chimes tinkle in
the breeze, is where your child's bones are buried.

I knew I had to get out and do something, not just in order

to expose the lies, but to stick up for Casey. I knew I also had to get up and do something to save myself from totally closing in upon myself and shrinking to nothing.

Shortly after he was killed, my sister made shirts with Casey's picture on them and they said "In Loving Memory. Casey Austin Sheehan. May 29, 1979 to April 4, 2004." Every time I wore the shirt I would be asked, "Who is that?"

"My son," I would reply.

"How did he die?" The person would ask with sincere sympathy in their voices.

"He was killed in the war," I would answer.

Nine times out of ten, the nominal American citizen would ask me in disbelief, "What war?"

"What war?!" my heart would scream, but I would say, "This war!" I wanted to yell, "What war do you think? People are dying in Iraq while you are shopping, drinking, eating, driving, fucking . . . whatever you are doing while people are dying and you don't even know that there is a war going on!"

In the first few weeks after Casey was killed we started to get to know the family of Sgt. Michael Mitchell, who was killed at 6:45 P.M., just eight minutes before Casey, in the same ambush.

Mike's sister, Christine, was trying to get in contact with the families of the eight soldiers killed in Sadr City in the ambush. I believe that we are the only two families of the soldiers killed that day who disagree with the war and with the president. In fact, a few of the families have gone on anti-Cindy tours speaking out against me.

I love these "Cindy doesn't speak for me" tours. The position of the Bush regime is so untenable that they can't answer the "Noble Cause" to support the war, so the various members of the tour have to attack me, a mother who has had her dear son killed for the lies and deceptions. But these tours happened way down the line of our struggle for peace.

The Mitchell family and the Sheehan family became close and joined in the struggle to end the war in Iraq. Bill, Mike's dad, and I became especially close and eventual cofounders of Gold Star Families for Peace. We have traveled all over the country together, and Bill has sometimes called himself my "bag boy." I remember so many times running through a train station or airport together with Bill alongside lugging my suitcase without complaint.

Bill was a single dad who raised Mike by himself since Mike was about eighteen months old. In the time that we have known each other, I have grown to feel like I know Mike and that he was my son, too.

Mike Mitchell was in the First Armored Division out of Germany and he had been in Iraq for almost a year on 04/04/04. The First A.D. was scheduled to leave Iraq a week after he was killed. As a matter of fact, the First Cav division had just taken control of Forward Operating Base War Eagle from the First A.D. at 6 P.M. that day—forty-five minutes before Mike was killed and fifty-three minutes before Casey was killed. Casey had been there only five days and Mike had only a week left.

Bill and I have both been told that Mike and Casey volunteered for the mission that killed them. We know our boys were each that kind of man, but we also know that the Army lies and that we will never really know what happened. The fact that the Army lies is fully evident in the Pat Tillman case. The Army told his family that he was killed by hostile fire and it turned out that one of his own men had killed him.

After I was fired from my job with the county at the end of July 2004 because of my frequent panic attacks, I became addicted to the Internet. I would go online early in the morning when I got up, and oftentimes I would find myself still in my jammies when the sun was going down. I was reading everything I could to belatedly educate myself on the lies of the war and about such things as the Project for the New American Century and the Carlyle Group. I was also hungry for news about Casey and his death day. One day I got an e-mail from Bill Mitchell that he had discovered a group called Military Families Speak Out (MFSO).

MFSO is a group of military families that was started by my now dear friends Charley Richardson and Nancy Lessin. Charley's son was in the Marines, and Charley and Nancy both opposed the invasion of Iraq and started MFSO as a way for all military families who oppose the war to join together. Charley and Nancy have been involved in union organizing for a long time. I felt a small ray of hope when Bill sent me to the website.

Carly and I joined MFSO and I wrote an e-mail to the website and included Carly's poem "A Nation Rocked to Sleep." I believe this act was the single moment in my life that started me on the road to activism.

Through MFSO, I met so many lovely people who had sons killed in Iraq. I met some people who lived to end the war and other people who would ultimately break my heart when it became obvious that their interest in the antiwar movement was to fuel their own egos and not so much to end the war. This was a tough lesson for me to learn, that not everybody has pure intentions.

When I started my quest to bring truth to the American public and to somehow make Casey's death count for something, I put everything I had into it. I used thousands of dollars of Casey's insurance money and spent weeks away from home. I slept on couches and floors, and in bus stations, airports, a bedroom in Connecticut that was also used as the old kitty's pee place, and a house in the Maine woods that I likened to the Unabomber's shack that didn't even have a lock on the bathroom door. I was also welcomed in some of the nicest homes that the peace movement could offer. I stayed in a mansion in Rhode Island once and I had my own bathroom there. I felt I was in "peace-activist heaven."

I left everything I knew and everyone I loved behind to try to stop others from being killed. It was and still is a very lonely existence, and the more I went out, the farther I traveled from my family and my old existence and friends. But I never did anything half-assed, and to me, this cause was too important not to give everything that I could to it. Casey and so many others had given everything—and I do mean *everything.*

I am telling you all this to explain why the Gold Star Families for Peace members who hurt me so badly were able to hurt me. The moms and other relatives who banded together to attack me were also doing great things for peace, but they became intensely jealous over the attention that I was getting. Soon after I began my journey, I was being invited to be on CNN, MSNBC, and other news networks. These invitations weren't about me, Cindy Sheehan; they came only because of the hard work I was willing to devote to the cause. Some of the other moms wanted what they perceived as the "glory" without having to sacrifice anything else to help end the war. I know the initial sacrifice of having a son killed is more than anyone should be asked for. I will write more about how the other moms not only abandoned me but actually bought into the smear machine as active participants during Camp Casey. I also believe that some of the people who joined Gold Star Families for Peace were agents provocateurs in the tradition of the golden Nixon years during the attacks on the anti–Vietnam War protestors.

In the first few months after 04/04/04, I met the other mom who was to form the nucleus of Gold Star Families for Peace with Dede, Bill Mitchell, and me: Jane Bright. Jane also lives in California with the rest of us. Her oldest son, Evan Ashcraft, was KIA in Iraq on July 24, 2003, at the age of twenty-four. The same age that Casey and Michael were. As a matter of fact, Evan was born exactly one week before Casey in 1979. I feel like Evan is my son also. Jane has been, and continues to be, the one person I turn to most consistently in my darkest moments. Evan was killed nine months before Casey, and Jane quickly became my "mentor in grief," which was immensely helpful, and I try to be that person for other moms who have so tragically and unfortunately come after me.

Jane, Bill, Dede, and I came together on July 4, 2004, at the Unitarian Universalist Church in Berkeley, California. MFSO had sent out a request for a speaker for a program at the church. Jane agreed to speak, and Bill, Dede, and I went there to support her. Jane brought her husband, Jim Bright, and the rest is history.

The synergy that we felt together was palpable. We all ended up speaking that day, and I wrote later that on that Fourth of July I broke my "slavery to silence." I found my voice and I have not lost it since.

Also in attendance at that church meeting was Deane Little, the person who founded RealVoices.org, which was a political action committee created to use real people to speak about how George Bush and his policies had harmed them and to work against him in the 2004 elections. Deane and his group filmed Jane Bright, Carly, and me in commercials that would push me into national prominence in the progressive peace movement.

One hot, hot day late in July, a filmmaker came over to our home in Vacaville to film commercials for RealVoices.org. Carly went first and read a powerful script with great strength. She talked about how much she missed her brother and how much George Bush and his policies had hurt her and our family. The commercials were filmed in black-and-white and were very well done. Carly's taping broke my heart. It is so tragic that when a mother buries a child and she still has other children, she hurts so much for them, too. But try as I might there was little I could do to comfort my other children, because I was in so much pain. In fact, I drew strength from them, when I should have been the one giving them strength—as mothers are supposed to do.

I had a script to read for my commercial but I remember just not "feeling it," so I threw my script away and just spoke from my heart for about three minutes, crying the entire time. I talked about how Bush lied to us about WMD and about the intelligence supporting the link between al Qaeda and Saddam, and how much it hurt to lose such a wonderful and honest son to such a pack of lies.

Apparently my commercial was very powerful, because MoveOn.org bought it from RealVoices.org to air in a two-million-dollar ad buy in swing states. MoveOn.org is a progressive website that, in 2004, had about two million members who contribute to progressive causes, including political campaigns. While MoveOn.org was tremendously helpful to us during Camp Casey in August, this high-profile commercial unfortunately caused a storm of resentment from some of the other families who had also filmed commercials for the PAC, and I think it was the beginning of many resentful feelings that would come to be directed at me.

Deane Little also didn't help ease the resentment but in fact fueled it after he sold the rights to my commercial to MoveOn.org for over $20,000. I think that it was because Deane began to get heat from the other families involved that he started an e-mail campaign against me. I was shocked and bewildered because I was not involved with the MoveOn people until afterward, and I could not help that they chose my commercial to air. It was a hint of things to come, though in retrospect I should have paid more attention to the resentment instead of sloughing it off as just hurt feelings that would be assuaged when Bush was defeated in the 2004 elections. It is so hard to judge my fellow grieving Gold Star Families when they are already going through so much, but I always marvel at how easily they can judge me, whether they agree with my antiwar stance or not!

After my commercial was purchased by MoveOn and broadcast in the swing states, I also got a taste of what the future held for me in terms of attacks from the right wing. It was the first time that I was accused of using my son's death for "political gain." This always baffles me. What am I gaining politically from what I am doing? I have always just wanted George Bush to be held accountable for his part in Casey's death.

I didn't campaign for John Kerry so much as I campaigned against George Bush. I did vote for John Kerry in the 2004 election, but just because he wasn't George Bush. As far as I was and still am concerned, Bonzo the Chimp—Ronald Reagan's old friend and costar—would be a better president than George W., which was hardly a good reason to endorse John Kerry. John Kerry was the new "lesser of two evils" who says he would have increased troop strength and that, knowing then what he knows now, he would still vote to give Bush the authority to invade Iraq. I will never make the mistake of supporting a pro-war Democrat again and am ashamed to say I ever did.

I was also given a glimpse of things to come when Pat's cousin's son called from one of the swing states where he was visiting with his new bride. This was a young man whom I babysat for a couple of years back when he and Casey were toddlers. He had seen my commercial on TV and called to say he was appalled that I would be saying such bad things about the poor president in a time of war. He is part of the contingent of "aunts, uncles, cousins, etc." who would write a nasty denunciation of me and offer glowing praise for the president while I was at Camp Casey less than a year later.

In October of 2004, after the MoveOn.org commercial was launched, Dede, Carly, Janey, Janey's best friend Janae, our friend Sabrina, and I went to D.C. to promote the commercial and to march in an antiwar rally with MFSO. The march began at the fountain at Arlington National Cemetery and ended in front of the White House. It was exactly six months since Casey was killed. And although we were all still in a state of shock, it was a very therapeutic few days for us.

We remembered how much fun we all always had together. How good it felt to laugh together, even though the laughter seemed a little forced and sometimes almost slightly deranged. Once, after getting up way too early, when we were driving up to join the start of the march in the parking lot of Arlington, Dede reached for an automated ticket, but the car window was closed and she banged her hand on the closed window. Oh, my God, we laughed so hard about that.

We met a lot of people that day whom I would become very

close to. There was Michael Berg, whose son, Nicholas, was a private contractor in Iraq. Not too long after Casey and Mike were killed, Nicholas was captured and beheaded by his captors, and his murder was shown on the Internet. I could never bring myself to watch the video, but I was so shocked for Nick's family. When I met Michael, I said, "Oh, my God, it was so hard to have Casey killed in Iraq, but when I heard what happened to Nick and to your family, I knew that there could be something worse than what happened to us."

Michael replied, "And when I met with some families whose loved ones were killed in 9/11 and they never found their bodies, I felt fortunate that at least we got both halves of Nick back to bury."

We both reflected on what a shitty world it was when one's own tragedy wasn't as bad as another's. It's still amazing to me that George Bush and his neocons could defile and demoralize our world so badly that I was actually a little bit comforted that at least Casey hadn't been captured and beheaded for the entire world to see!

Also on that march I met Lila Lipscomb, who was featured in Michael Moore's movie *Fahrenheit 9/11.* Lila is a dear woman who had supported our young people going into the military until her son was killed in Iraq and she learned of the treachery of our government. She and I became good friends and she became another "mentor" to me in my grief. Her stance against the war and her appearance in Michael Moore's movie cost her dearly, and she was very brave and humble to allow her story to be broadcast for millions of people all over the world to see. I actually saw the movie with her in San Francisco, and she was able to warn me when I needed to leave the theater because some hard parts showing the fighting in Iraq were coming up. When Andy went to see the movie shortly after it came out, he came home and sat on my lap and sobbed and said, "If I had seen that movie before we met George Bush, I would be in jail right now because I would have punched him."

When Janey's boyfriend, Daniel, saw *Fahrenheit 9/11,* he also came to me and hugged me and sobbed and kept apologizing over and over again for his dad voting for George Bush. I wish the movie had come out sooner—I believe it would have definitely turned the tide against George Bush. I think Michael has expressed similar regrets. But people like my in-laws despise Michael Moore almost as much as they despise me, while refusing even to see the movie. Ignorance breeds ignorance.

I also met the kids (they hate it when I call them that, but anyone under thirty years of age is a "kid" to me!) of Iraq Veterans Against the War (IVAW). These young men and women would come to be parts of my heart and my partners in activism, and it has been wonderful to see their ranks grow from a couple of dozen in October 2004 to a couple of hundred currently. Most of them call me Mom, and when I have talked with them individually about Casey's death in the war, they have almost always said, "I am so sorry. I wish it were me." That always breaks my heart because, first of all, they love their fellow soldiers so much that they are all willing to take their places and die for them and, secondly, that what they saw and had to do to survive in Iraq was so horrible many of them would rather be dead than alive. So many of them came to support me at Camp Casey, and they have all told me that being there helped heal their inner wounds and that they hoped that if they had come home in a flag-draped coffin that their moms would have done the same things that I did.

Speaking of right-wing attacks, I just have to interrupt writing this chapter to answer an attack by Republican congressman Jack Kingston, who called me a "nutcase" in a congressional committee meeting yesterday. I am going to include his press release here, as well as my response, as an example of what I am constantly up against. Here is the press release from the congressman's office:

FROM: **Kingston Press Office**
<u>**Kingston.Press.Office@mail.house.gov**</u>
DATE: **March 31, 2006 11:44:45 AM EST**
TO:
SUBJECT: **SHEEHAN IS A NUTCASE / KINGSTON V. LIBERALS**

JACK'S BLOG
Cindy Sheehan IS A "Nutcase" March 31st,
2006 by Press Staff

In today's CongressDailyAM (full story after the jump due to subscription), Sue Davis reports that Congressman Kingston got into a "discussion" yesterday in a closed-door meeting with two liberal Democrats regarding anti-war beatnik, Cindy Sheehan.

A closed hearing of the House Defense Appropriations Subcommittee turned contentious Thursday as Rep. Jack Kingston, R-Ga., Subcommittee ranking member Jack Murtha, D-Pa., and others sparred over the meaning of anti-war activist Cindy Sheehan, heroes and military service.

According to one Democratic source present at the hearing, Kingston commented that Sheehan was "a nutcase" and lamented that too many of the human interest stories coming out of the war in Iraq center on anti-war activists like Sheehan and filmmaker Michael Moore and do not give proper service to heroic tales of U.S. soldiers.

"Who would argue that Cindy Sheehan's son is not a hero? I mean, come on," he said, chalking the exchange up to election-year politics.

"I think she is a very flaky woman," Kingston told CongressDaily. "I think we need more heroes. The only people that get press are people like Moore and Sheehan."

Cindy Sheehan is a nutcase. In fact, you may remember Cindy Sheehan from her recent trip to Venezuela for the World Social Forum where she met with Venezuela's anti-American leftist president, Hugo Chavez (pictured above).

Or you may recall how she refers to the terrorists who are killing American soldiers in Iraq as "freedom fighters." Check out this story by WorldNetDaily for more. The problem is that what Howard Dean famously termed the "democratic wing of the Democratic Party" has now completely taken over.

And here is my reply:

Congressman Kingston,

How dare you psychoanalyze me and call me a "nutcase"! How dare you call me a beatnik and lie about me in your blog!

First of all, April 4th, 2006, this upcoming Tuesday will be the 2nd anniversary of my son's death. Casey Austin Sheehan was a man filled with integrity and courage. He was a hero who never backed down from the right thing his entire life. He was an amazing person who did not hide when his commander in chief sent him to a war based on lies even when he knew they were lies. He carried out his duty, unlike his commander in chief who went AWOL from the Alabama Air National Guard (woo . . . tough duty), and he volunteered to serve his country, unlike the vice-commander in chief who had "other priorities" during the Vietnam War. I am not against anyone getting out of that generation's mistake of a war, but to illegitimately come to power when they grew up and send an entire new generation off to fight, die and kill innocent people in their own war of choice for greed in unconscionable. I hope I am not using too big words for you.

Second of all, I have never called "terrorists" freedom fighters. I have called the resistance fighters who killed Casey such, but they are fighting to get the occupying forces out of their country and have a legitimate right to wage a resistance against occupiers. I don't like that they are killing our children, for God's sake, they killed my oldest child; my sweet and wonderful Casey. However, our government is committing war crimes and crimes against humanity against the people of Iraq. Have you heard of white phosphorous? Have you heard of torture? Have you heard of Abu Ghraib and Guantánamo? Have you heard about our Constitution and the Geneva Conventions?

Have you also heard that Saddam had nothing to do with the tragedy of 9/11 and that he had no WMD? How can you support a liar and his policies that are draining our precious life blood, depleting our military, sucking our treasury dry, and have harmed almost beyond repair the people and land of the Gulf States from Hurricane Katrina? Have you heard that Osama bin Laden is still at large and two countries, Iraq and Afghanistan, that had nothing to do with 9/11 are devastated, and I hope they can recover from George's brand of "freedom and democracy."

As to your having a problem with my meeting with Hugo Chavez, who survived a coup that was orchestrated by the Bush administration and has been democratically elected to his office eight times, you can't pick and choose to support only the democracies that agree with George Bush. I don't support everything that President Chavez stands for, but his people love him and he is truly trying to make the lot better for the 80 percent of the people who were in poverty when he took over and has reduced that figure to 37 percent. He is stealing from the rich to help the poor when George Bush and his policies do the opposite. Hugo Chavez is not anti-American—he is anti–George Bush, and I have to agree with him on that. He has provided low-cost heating fuel to underprivileged citizens in our own country and has donated at least $40,000.00 to the various aid organizations in the Gulf States.

Did you have a problem with George Bush kissing the sheik from Saudi Arabia when sixteen of the terrorists that flew airplanes into our buildings on 9/11 came from Saudi Arabia? Did you have a problem with Donald Rumsfeld shaking Saddam's hand and selling him weapons that are now killing our children in Iraq? Do you have a problem with the fact that since your party's devastating invasion of Iraq, the so-called "Axis of Evil" have become more powerful and even more dangerous to America? Did you have a problem with George Bush wanting to sell our ports to Dubai when they are one of the only countries on earth that recognize the Taliban? Did you have a problem with the bin Laden family being flown out of the United States days after 9/11 when our own citizens could not fly and many of us were trapped far from our homes ourselves? Did you have a problem with George, et al., ignoring all of the intelligence reports before 9/11 that said that terrorists were planning on "flying airplanes" into our buildings?

I am not a left-wing Democrat, and I hold many of the members of that party as responsible as I hold your party and George Bush and his administration. I do not think that there is anything political about an illegal and immoral war.

Our country was founded on dissent and on the blood of "freedom fighters." I have every right to be doing what I am doing to try and stop the needless and unnecessary killing without being wrongly judged by you. I believe that you and anyone else who would deny me, and Michael Moore for that matter, our rights and responsibilities as patriotic Americans are the ones who are un-American and traitors to the American way of life. A member of your own party and noted warmonger Theodore Roosevelt said:

"Patriotism means to stand by the country. It does not mean to stand by the president or any other public official, save exactly to the degree in which he himself stands by the country. It is patriotic to support him insofar as he efficiently serves the country. It is unpatriotic not to oppose him to the exact extent that by inefficiency or otherwise he fails in his duty to stand by the country. In either event, it is unpatriotic not to tell the truth, whether about the president or anyone else."

George Bush has admitted that Saddam had no WMD or ties to al Qaeda. He has admitted to spying on Americans without due process and has called the Constitution an "old scrap of paper." He is responsible for the tragic deaths of thousands of people and for America losing its reputation in the international community and to support his failed presidency is not only unpatriotic as Teddy said, but also a war crime.

I am not a nutcase and I am not an unpatriotic war criminal like you and others who still support the most failed presidency in the history of our country.

What I am is a devastated, broken-hearted mother who will mourn the needless death of my son for the rest of my life. I just want the killing to stop before there are any more American or Iraqi Casey and Cindy Sheehans.

Peace soon,

Cindy Sheehan

One thing I have learned on my journey is that if you love our country but hate what our government is doing, you are labeled "un-American" and a "nutcase," but if you let your son be killed in a useless war and are obediently silent about it, then you are the "Mother of a Hero." I am the mother of a hero—as a matter of fact, I am the mother of four heroes and nothing, or no one, can take that away from me, not even an ignorant congressman.

Anyway, where was I?

The Sheehan family (and countless others) worked hard to defeat George Bush in the 2004 elections, but he "won" anyway and we were pretty devastated. Our family felt betrayed by the American people who seemed to support George and his killing of innocent Americans and Iraqis. We felt that our country had abandoned Casey and the rest of us. We were depressed and felt as if we'd been kicked in the stomach anew. My three wonderful and courageous children encouraged dozens of their friends to register and vote for the first time, and they were all incredibly disappointed with the results and the seeming uselessness of their first votes. I couldn't stay discouraged or even admit that all of my hard work was for nothing, so two days after the elections, I wrote an open letter to George Bush and sent it to my e-mail list, including the office of the president and the vice president—I wonder if anyone close to them read it and dismissed it as the rantings of a grieving mother?

In the letter, I promised him that I would take on the mandate of the more than fifty-nine million people who did not vote for him. I would hold him accountable for Casey's death and fight to have him impeached for lying to the world and to the country.

That day in the seventh month of my mourning, which many people consider the beginning of the most difficult period of mourning a child, holding George and his administration accountable for what they did to the world became my life's work.

The seventh month of mourning is about the time when the numbing sense of shock starts to wear off and you are overcome with the real, undiluted pain of your loss. I remember walking around the house in those days, just picking things up and putting them down and crying, and crying, and crying.

The ninth month was also incredibly arduous for me because I kept on thinking about the first months of Casey's existence, before I even knew he was Casey. In those days, we didn't take automatic tests to find out if there were any anomalies or what gender the baby was. We just waited until the birth to see if we had a boy or girl. Being in the womb has often been described as another world and birth as a death to that world. Casey was protected and fed by me in my womb for nine months, then he was dragged out kicking and screaming. Casey was protected and fed by me for twenty-one years until he went into the Army. Even after that, I tried my hardest to protect him and enjoyed cooking for him when he came home. Then he was violently jerked from this world and sent to the next. On January 4, 2005, Casey had completed his first nine months buried in the cold womb of our mother earth, and it was so freaking hard for me to endure that day: even harder than other days.

While I was trying to live my life without Casey in it, I had a brainstorm: since I knew so many other people in the same circumstances who felt the same way that I did about the war and about George and the other neocons, I would start a group made up of those same people. On January 20, 2005, Jane Bright, Bill Mitchell, Dede Miller, I, and a few others launched Gold Star Families for Peace.

Not only did we come together to expose the lies and end the war before too many more families had to join our wretched ranks, but also to be a support group for each other even after the troops come home. Because when we do prevail, and we will prevail, and our troops do come home, our loved ones will still be dead. We will need each other for the rest of our lives.

We are a unique group because we count among our members people who have had a loved one killed in every war since and including World War II. It is comforting, but also heartbreaking, to know mothers, fathers, sisters, brothers, aunts, uncles, and children of people who have been dead for years but who still grieve as if their loved ones had died yesterday. It is comforting that families do go on, children are born, and people never forget their dead loved ones and hold them in their hearts forever.

Our very first action as members of our new group was to try to get a meeting with Secretary of Defense Donald Rumsfeld. That was back in January 2005, and as of this writing, we still have not been granted an audience with him. We have even had members of Congress implore him on our behalf for a meeting. We decided that since he wouldn't meet with us, then we would go to him.

Five members of GSFP, including Bill and me, supported by members of Military Families Speak Out (MFSO), including Nancy and Charley, Veterans for Peace (VFP), and Iraq Veterans Against the War (IVAW) convened in Lady Bird Johnson Park adjacent to the Pentagon on a freezing cold, snowy, January morning on the day before the inauguration. The thing I remember most about that day, besides being stopped by about two dozen Pentagon security guards and D.C. police before we got to the Pentagon parking lot, was the snot running out of my nose and freezing on my face from the bitter cold. I had on a jacket, gloves, stocking cap, boots, and long underwear, but still I was frozen stiff and miserable. I held a baby picture of Casey and made a statement about the fact that Rummy would not meet with the families of the very people whom his policies had killed in Iraq.

The next morning, after our Pentagon action had garnered some international attention, I was invited to appear live on *Good Morning America,* broadcasting from the Library of Congress on the morning of King George's second inaugural. I spoke out in opposition to the millions of dollars that were being spent on the inappropriate gala when our young people were still in Iraq and, while fighting, dying, and killing innocent people, still didn't have proper equipment, body armor, enough food and water. After I was on, the First Lady came on and said that they did too support the troops. Why, they'd just had a ball in their honor the night before!

I was on live with Diane Sawyer and I met the dying Peter Jennings, who was a very gracious man. He made sure to introduce himself to me and expressed his condolences for Casey's death. While Diane and I were doing the interview, the director was talking nonstop in our earplug and we could hear his directions to the crew. After the interview, Diane immediately leaned over to me and said: "My God, you are amazing. How did you do that?"

"I had four kids in six years. I buried my oldest. That was nothing," I remember replying.

That morning, while I was waiting for the driver to take me back to the freezing cold house where I was staying during this D.C. trip, I again ran into Senator John McCain, who also denies what he said to me that day.

I was waiting in the Green Room and in walked the senator. I said, "Hi, you probably don't remember me, but I met you at Fort Lewis, Washington, last June and I encouraged you to run as John Kerry's running mate." He claimed remembering that I had asked him to do that. (And still does.)

I then told him what I had been doing to end the war, and he said this to me: "You keep doing what you are doing. America needs to hear your voice." I promised him that I would. However, when I met with him in D.C. last September, he denied ever having said this to me, stating, "I support the president and this war, why would I say something like that?" I used to respect John McCain so highly! I wish he would remember his roots as a soldier and when he was an honorable man and quit bending over for George and the Republican Party! I believe he is a disgrace.

After I cofounded GSFP, I think I became the busiest peace activist on the face of the planet. After thinking that I was cold in D.C., I traveled to Maine for a week, and that's when I stayed with a virtual stranger in the "Unabomber shack" with the unlockable bathroom door. My host was a nice man, but I didn't know that we would be alone together in Middle-of-Nowhere, Maine, and that it would be about thirty below zero for that week. I was so upset with him and, irrationally, I know, with all the people who would choose to live in Maine in January. When I would express my unreasonable anger at the sweet, but slightly screwy, citizens of Maine, they would wonder aloud if it ever snowed in California. I would retort, "Sure, it snows in California. But we don't live where it snows, and we don't allow it to snow where we live." However, even when I have been up at resorts in California when it was snowing, it is never as cold as it was when I was in Maine in January.

I was invited back to Maine to be a featured speaker at an outdoor event the next July (right before I left for Camp Casey), and I realized why they lived there and absolved the good people of the state of Maine for living there in January. Maine in July is worth all of the other months put together!

In May of that year, after having traveled far and wide in the country speaking to increasingly larger and more pissed-off audiences, GSFP became one of the first organizations to sign onto the After Downing Street Coalition. This eventually led to my testifying in a small basement room of the Capitol for Congressman John Conyers at the Downing Street Memo hearings.

When I read the Downing Street Memos, I was stunned. To me they were proof positive that George lied, and that he knew he was lying about the reasons for the invasion of Iraq. I thought that the exposure of the memos and the subsequent outcry would be the "tipping point" against the war and the Bush administration. I thought that millions of Americans would rise up and demand that the troops be withdrawn from Iraq immediately so no one else would be killed for the tragic duplicity. I thought America would demand the resignation of George Bush and everyone who lied to the American people and to the world.

Well, my expectations for the outrage that should have occurred from the exposure of the memos and the hearings didn't materialize. I was so devastated and discouraged, this was my low point in the struggle. I was even more depressed after the seeming failure of the Downing Street hearings than I was after the seeming failure of the 2004 elections.

We in the After Downing Street Coalition tried so hard. Among those who testified were Joe Wilson, who exposed the lie about the yellow-cake uranium assertions and whose wife was in turn exposed by high-level members of BushCo; Ray

McGovern, a twenty-seven-year analyst for the CIA who testi-fied on the faulty intelligence; John Bonifaz, who is a lawyer with expertise in the Constitution; and me—who testified to the human cost of the lies surrounding our entry into the war.

The one good thing that came from the hearings was that I got to be fast friends with the other witnesses and the members of the After Downing Street Coalition, and we have done some amazing work together since. The work we did for the coalition was also one more drop in the bucket for bringing a case for im-peachment in front of the American people. If we can't do it all in one day, we will do it drop by drop.

I was also given another preview of what I could expect from the right-wing smear machine when I went to Camp Casey. They were all over this one! We four witnesses were lumped to-gether and called every name in the book including "wingnuts" by such credible commentators as drug addict Rush Limbaugh. "Wingnuts!" A former ambassador, a former CIA employee, a respected attorney from Boston, and a mother of a war hero. A more rabid bunch of wingnuts never were and never will be as-sembled in one place ever again!

In closing this first chapter of my struggle against the war, the war machine, and the Bush administration, I would like to offer the testimony I gave to the Conyers commission on June 16, 2005. That was less than two months before I decided to take matters into my own hands and head down to Crawford, Texas.

This is the testimony that I thought was going to rock the country and raise a hue and cry that would be the next "shot heard around the world."

Congressman Conyers and all, it is an honor to be here to testify about the effect that the revelations of the Downing Street Memo have had on me and my family. It is an honor that I wish never had to happen. I believe that not any of us should be gathered here today for this reason: as the result of an invasion/occupation that never should have occurred.

My son, Spc. Casey Austin Sheehan, was KIA in Sadr City, Baghdad, on 04/04/04. He was in Iraq for only two weeks before L. Paul Bremer inflamed the Shi'ite militia into a rebellion which resulted in the deaths of Casey and six other brave soldiers who were tragically killed in an ambush. Bill Mitchell, the father of Sgt. Mike Mitchell, who was one of the other soldiers killed that awful day, is with us here. This is a picture of Casey when he was seven months old. It's an enlargement of a picture he carried in his wallet until the day he was killed. He loved this picture of himself. It was returned to us with his personal effects from Iraq. . . . How many of you have seen your child in his/her premature coffin? It is a shocking and very painful sight. . . . The most tragic irony is that if the Downing Street Memo proves to be true, Casey and thousands of people should still be alive.

I believed before our leaders invaded Iraq in March 2003, and I am even more convinced now, that this aggression on Iraq was based on a lie of historic proportions and was blatantly unnecessary. The so-called Downing Street Memo dated 23 July, 2003, only confirms what I already suspected: the leadership of this country rushed us into an illegal invasion of another sovereign country on prefabricated and cherry-picked intelligence. Iraq was no threat to the United States of America, and the devastating sanctions and bombing raids against Iraq were working. As a matter of fact, in interviews in 1999 with respected journalist and longtime Bush family friend, Mickey Herskowitz, then–Governor George Bush stated: "One of the keys to being seen as a great leader is to be seen as a commander in chief. My father had all this political capital built up when he drove the Iraqis out of Kuwait and he wasted it. If I have a chance to invade. . . . if I had that much capital, I'm not going to waste it. I'm going to get everything passed that I want to get passed and I'm going to have a successful presidency." It looks like George Bush was ready to lead this country into an avoidable war even before he became president.

From the exposé of the Downing Street Memo and the conversations with George Bush from 1999, it seems like the invasion of Iraq and the deaths of so many innocent people were preordained. It appears that my boy Casey was given a death sentence even before he joined the Army in May of 2000.

When a president lies to Congress and the American people, it is a serious offense. If the Downing Street Memo proves to be true, then it would appear that the president, vice president, and many members of the cabinet deceived the world before the invasion of Iraq. As the result of this alleged lie, over 1,700 brave young Americans who were only trying to do their duties have come home in flag-draped coffins: images, as if they were ashamed of our children, our leaders won't even let the American people see; thousands upon thousands of Iraqis who were guilty only of the crime of living in Iraq are dead; thousands of our young people will go through the rest of their lives missing one or more limbs, and too many will come home missing parts of their souls and humanity.

Kevin Lucey, who found his Marine son, Jeffrey, who was recently home from Iraq, hanging dead from a garden hose in his basement wrote to me:

"We ask daily where was the urgency; where was the necessity of rushing in. Can anyone explain to us, to his mother, and to his father as to why he felt that he had to die by his own hand. Why are the ones in position of power so afraid to ask people like us to discuss what happened to Jeff? Jeff can teach us so much. This war was so misguided and had so many other agendas which had nothing to do with the country."

Kevin, who cradled his son when he was his sweet baby boy, cradled Jeff's lifeless body for the last time in his arms after he cut him down from the hose. The Jeff that the Luceys saw march off to a reckless war was not the one who limped home. The Jeff his family knew died in Iraq, murdered by the inhumanity of gratuitous war.

The deceptions and betrayals that led to the U.S. invasion and occupation of Iraq cost my family a price too dear to pay and almost too much to bear: the precious and young life of Casey. Casey was a good soldier who loved his family, his community, his country, and his God. He was trustworthy and trusting, and the leadership of his country seemingly betrayed him. He was an indispensable part of our family. An obedient, sweet, funny, and loving son to myself and his father, Pat, and an adored big brother to his sisters, Carly and Jane, and his brother Andy. And the beloved nephew to my sister, Auntie, who is here with me today. Our family has been devastated and torn asunder by his murder.

I believe that the reasons that we citizens of the United States of America were given for the invasion of Iraq have unequivocally been proven to be false. I also believe that Casey and his buddies have been killed to line the pockets of already wealthy people and to feed the insatiable war machine that has always devoured our young. Casey died saving his buddies, and I know so many of our brave young soldiers died doing the same thing: but he and his fellow members of the military should never have been sent to Iraq. I know the family of Sgt. Sherwood Baker, who was killed guarding a team that was looking for the mythic WMDs in Baghdad. The same WMDs that were the justification for invading Iraq as outlined in the Downing Street Memo. Sherwood's brother, Dante Zappala, and his dad, Al Zappala, are here with us today. I believe the Downing Street Memo proves that our leaders betrayed too many innocents into an early grave. The lives of the ones left behind are shattered almost beyond repair.

I also believe an investigation into the Downing Street Memo is completely warranted and the necessary first step into righting the wrong that is Iraq and holding someone accountable for the needless, senseless, and avoidable deaths of many thousands. As far as I am concerned, it doesn't matter if one is a Democrat or a Republican, a full investigation into the veracity of the Downing Street Memo must be initiated immediately. Casey was not asked his political affiliation before he was sent to die in Iraq. The innocent people who are having their blood shed by the bucketsful in Iraq don't even know or care what American partisan politicking is all about. Every minute that we waste in gathering signatures on petitions, or arguing about partisan politics, more blood is being spilled in Iraq. How many more families here in America are going to get the visit from the Grim Reaper dressed in a U.S. military uniform while we are trying to get our congressional leadership to do their duties to the Constitution and to the people of America? I believe that Congress expediently abrogated their constitutional responsibility to declare war when they passed the War Powers Act, and they bear at least some responsibility for the needless heartache wrought on this world by our government. I believe that supporting a full investigation into the Downing Street Memo is a good beginning for Congress to redeem itself for abandoning the Constitution and the American people.

There are too many stories of heartache and loss to tell at a hearing like this. I have brought testimonies of other families who have been devastated by the war. Their soldiers' names are: Sgt. Sherwood Baker, KIA 04/26/04; 1st Lt. Neil Santoriello, KIA 08/13/04; Sgt. Mike Mitchell, KIA 04/04/04; Spc. Casey Sheehan, also KIA 04/04/04; Lt. Jeff Kaylor, KIA 04/07/03; Spc. Kevin S. K. Wessell, KIA 04/19/05; Spc. Jonathan Castro, KIA 12/21/04; PFC William Prichard, KIA 02/11/04; Spc. Joseph Blickenstaff, KIA 12/08/03, and 1st Lt. Kenneth Ballard, KIA 05/30/04. I would like to have the testimonies put into the record and recorded for all to read the words of boundless love, bottomless loss, and deep despair.

There are a few people around the United States and a couple of my fellow witnesses who were a little justifiably worried that in my anger and anguish over Casey's premeditated death, I would use some swear words, as I have been known to do on occasion when speaking about the subject. Mr. Conyers, out of my deep respect for you, the other representatives here, my fellow witnesses, and viewers of these historic proceedings, I was able to make it through an entire testimony without using any profanity. However, if anyone deserves to be angry and use profanity, it is I. What happened to Casey and humanity because of the apparent dearth of honesty in our country's leadership is so profane that it defies even my vocabulary skills. We as Americans should be offended more by the profanity of the actions of this administration than by swear words. We have all heard the old adage that actions speak louder than words, and for the sake of Casey and our other precious children, please hold someone accountable for their actions and their words of deception.

Again, I would like to thank you for inviting me to testify today and giving me a chance to tell my story, which is the tragic story of too many families here in the

U.S. and in Iraq. I hope and pray that this is the first step in exposing the lies to the light and bringing justice for the ones who can no longer speak for themselves. More importantly, I hope this is a step in bringing our other children home from the lie of historic proportions that is Iraq. Thank you.

The hearings in that small basement room of the Capitol were historic, but they weren't the catalyst that changed the country. I had no idea then what the catalyst would be, or that I would be a spark that helped to light the fire of antiwar sentiment in this country, but we would all find out shortly!

Chapter 8

Death of the Sheehan Family

"But we still together . . ."

—CASEY SHEEHAN

IN RETROSPECT, THE SHEEHAN FAMILY HAD BEGUN to fall apart even before Casey died.

There was a TV show starring the Wayans family called *In Living Color.* It was a very clever show. One of the stars was a practically unknown Jim Carrey. The show had a regular sketch about an old black couple who had been married for many decades. The old couple would have visitors and they would pretend to be lovey-dovey while their guests were there. The visitor would remark how amazing it was that they had been married for so long, and in unison the couple would say, "And we still together."

Then, as soon as the visitors would leave, the couple would get into a knock-down, drag-out fight! Every time Pat and I would fight, Casey would look up from whatever he was doing, or pass by the room and say, "And we still together." That would always make Pat and me laugh and defuse the situation a little.

By the time our firstborn, our dear, sweet, funny, and loving boy, was killed on April 4, 2004, our marriage, I believe, was not sick, but stagnant and moored in the place of comfort instead of happiness; complacency instead of excitement; ennui instead of love. We fought pretty much constantly, but I thought since our marriage was better than my parents' marriage, that it was a good one.

For the first few weeks after Casey was killed, Pat and I would lie in bed in the morning before we got up and hold each other and cry. We would be up about an hour before the throngs of people would descend on our home to fix us breakfast and help us get on with the task of life after a shocking death. That was when I believed that the intimacy would return to our marriage and we would grow closer. I thought Casey's death would save our family. I was wrong.

As I have stated before, I was a horrible mother to my other three children after Casey was killed. It seemed that they had to spend all of their time comforting me. I was in such a dark place of pain and regret that I could not even begin to be a mother to them. I resented the people who would say to me, "You need to pull yourself out of this. You have three other children." Or, "At least you have three more." As if Casey were a lost family pet that could be replaced by another.

Of course I have three other children, and I am so grateful

that I do—I really think I was able to resist committing suicide after Casey died because of them. I am so grateful that I have strong and compassionate children, but having them did not make up for Casey being dead. I would feel exactly the same way if any one of them had died instead of Casey. For the eighteen years since Janey was born, I was the mother of four. For twenty-four years I was the mother of Casey. If a person has to have a limb amputated, do other people tell them, "At least you have three other limbs!" Really, I hope I have never been so hurtful to anybody, but with all of our good intentions, I probably have been.

In the months after, I could see that we were relying too much on Carly to hold the family together, and while she took on that role for a while, it was starting to put a strain on her. One day she sent me an e-mail that said, "I am alive." I felt awful, but powerless to help her. I felt guilty but was still nursing my stump from my amputation, which was still so raw. Even today, I still feel like a mother of four, and it is such a rude awakening not to be. I still call Carly my "oldest daughter" when she is, in fact, my oldest child and now older than Casey was when he was killed. I can't help but resist the fact that I am missing a vital part of me, and I dread the day when Janey hits twenty-five and she is older than eternally age-twenty-four Casey. From that point on, Casey will be the baby of the family, and that is not a natural thing.

Andy also changed direction in his life from being mildly irresponsible to wanting to be just like his big brother. He became the model son and the model citizen. He started going back to mass and helping with the parish youth ministry like Casey did. He stopped arguing with his dad and just being an all-around grumpy pest. And he did this all without any resentment or reservation. He still can cry very openly for Casey and talks about him all the time. He went from being my least stable child to being my most stable, and I can't tell him enough how proud I am of him.

I am not saying that it wasn't a struggle, and isn't still a struggle, for Andy and me. He wants to support what I do without any reservations, and he wants me to come back home and be with his dad again. We have had some huge fights over this, but at least Andy is willing to express his anger at me and about the divorce and we can talk it out.

Janey is the one I worry the most about. Darling Janey, the baby of the family who has been adored and coddled her entire life. Casey used to carry her to bed every night and tell her bedtime stories. One night Janey was lying on a blanket in the front yard staring at the stars. I went out to talk to her and this is what she said to me:

I wish I was able to talk to the media about Casey. I would tell them that when he was around me, he talked a lot, and goofed off, and teased me, and he was really funny. I would tell them that he was the best big brother ever and I miss him more every day. I would tell them that I used to hold his feet down so he could do sit-ups and every time he sat up he would kiss me.

Janey and Casey cherished each other, but she can't cry for

him. She has never been able to cry, even when she was physically hurt. When she was two she fell down and split her chin open and I could see her stubborn will exerting itself and forcing her not to cry. I wish this for my baby doll: that she be able to cry and cry and cry for her brother. Not being able to cry is one problem that I have never had!

Fortunately I have been able to be more of a mother again to my other children as time goes on. But first I had to redefine for myself what being a mother means. The four of us struggled for many months with redefining not only what being the new Sheehan family meant, but also what our new rolls were. Carly went from being the oldest daughter to being the oldest; Andy from being the youngest son to the only son; Janey was still the baby, but her touchstone was gone.

One of the reasons why Pat and I are no longer together is that he wanted to go back to the old Sheehan family that existed prior to 04/04/04; I knew, even before I was an "international peace sensation," that that was not going to be possible. No matter how Pat struggled to maintain a sense of normalcy, I would never again feel normal.

On 04/04/04 my entire life was not only turned upside down and inside out but sideways. It was torn asunder from every point of view. I could not ever be the Cindy Lee Miller Sheehan who existed before Casey was killed. I knew, however, that I could be better.

I went from being the mom who did everyone's laundry, packed lunches, kissed boo-boos, tucked in at night, cleaned up everyone's messes, to being someone who fights for all of humanity's children, not just her own.

I went from being the mom whose life revolved around her children to the one who had a life separate from her children but remained intimately connected to them.

I think I am a better mom because I am free from trying to be society's ideal mom. I know that I am a deeply flawed person who owes her children, and especially Casey, an apology for trying only to live up to the world's expectations, and not to her own integrity.

Which brings me to a second reason why Pat and I are no longer together: I knew that I had somehow let Casey down by allowing him to join the military and to march off to a war that we, as a family, knew was wrong. I knew that if I was going to go on a path to hold someone accountable for Casey's death, then I would have to face my own part in it.

I believe that regrets, introspection, and retrospection should be part of the normal process of grieving. I instantly had survivor guilt after Casey was killed. How could I still be alive when my child was dead? How is such a thing even possible? But I also knew that when I was a young child, our country was embroiled in an ugly, unnecessary war that was built and sustained on lies. I was a history student. I knew our country rarely goes to war for anything but to feed the military-industrial complex. I knew our so-called leaders rarely, if ever, had our best interests in mind when they did anything. I knew that our government was by the rich and for the rich; yet in 2000 I had been lulled into a false sense of complacency and peace during the Clinton regime.

If I had bothered to look farther than the end of my own nose and past trying to pay the monthly bills and keep the Sheehan family up with the "Joneses," I would have seen that Bill Clinton got our country into needless wars and innocent people were killed in the war crimes that his administration committed.

If I wasn't so busy watching the boob tube for my entertainment, I would have known that our country was supporting ruinous sanctions against Iraq that killed over five hundred thousand Iraqi children and over five hundred thousand Iraqi adults. I would have known that the United States was bombing "strategic" targets in Iraq all during the nineties—and I would have cared if I had known. I have never supported killing, but in retrospect, apparently I didn't even want to know about it.

If I had read General Butler's *War Is a Racket*, I NEVER would have given even the slightest support to the military or thought that it was a good and honorable thing to join to defend the country, because I would have known that war is always a racket, the oldest racket, and there would have been never even a question of any of my kids enlisting. I can, incredibly, remember once even encouraging Carly to enlist in the Air Force so they would pay for her to go to med school. And she almost did join the Navy with her best friend Adrianna, but was denied entry, thank the Goddess, because she has a detectable heart murmur.

Yes, before I could blame George Bush, or the media, or Congress, or the American people, for Casey's death, I had to realize that I also had quite of bit of my dear boy's blood on my own hands.

It was so difficult for me to realize that Casey was killed for lies. But it was even more distressing to eventually realize that I (albeit unknowingly) lied to him and shirked my duties as a responsible parent. I spent many days in a funk of depression and gloom. I was praying to Casey for forgiveness and, frankly, frightening Pat, who was not ready to also claim accountability for Casey's death.

Pat insisted and still insists that Casey was a grown man who made fully aware and conscious decisions when he enlisted and reenlisted and "volunteered" to go on the mission that killed him. I believe that Casey made uninformed, immature, and brainwashed decisions. I take full responsibility for that, and now I feel that BushCo also needs to accept blame and responsibility for their part.

The depth of my despair over the months frightened Pat badly. My full-throttle, balls-to-the-wall approach to try to rectify things and save other lives not only scared him, but he resented being reminded on a daily basis that Casey had been unjustly killed. As I said before, Pat wanted to go back to pre–04/04/04 and I wouldn't allow him to do that, because I couldn't do it myself.

We grew apart, and the fire that fueled our separation was the fact that we each grieved differently. I resented it when Pat was able to go through parts of his day without dwelling on Casey the way I did, and do, every minute. I resented it when Pat told me I needed to "get a hobby" so I could get on with my life. As if I ever could, or can.

I resented him. I just resented him. And I know that he loved his son more than his own life and would gladly have traded places with him, but I resented the fact that he wouldn't take responsibility for Casey's death and he wouldn't grant me the forgiveness that I needed for my shame. Right or wrong, I wanted him to acknowledge it, own it, and work through it. I now know I was the unreasonable one and Pat needed the space to work things out for himself.

I was very selfish in my mourning, claiming the most grief. I was the champion griever, and I couldn't be consoled or talked out of my sadness. I wore my grief like a burial shroud and I resented anyone who tried to come between it and me.

I can't say I was right or wrong, though. I never wanted to walk in the ugly shoes that were cobbled for me by George Bush and the war machine. But I knew I had to walk in them my way.

The Sheehan family did die with Casey—the family of six who never wanted to be apart for too long. The family who would all pile in whatever junky car we owned at the time just to go out for frozen yogurt. Whenever I did have to travel and be away from my family, I would be so homesick that Pat and I would talk on the phone for hours before I fell asleep. Likewise when Pat had to go on business trips (even though I slept better when he was gone, because he snored).

We had problems before Casey died, yes, but I think if we hadn't buried one of our children so very prematurely, we would still be together and Casey would still be lovingly teasing us when we fought. Oh God, how I wish it were so!

The Sheehan family is dead. Long live the new, redefined Sheehan family.

Somehow, some way, we will make it.

Chapter 9

We're Going to Crawford

*The families of the fallen can rest assured that their
loved ones died for a noble cause.*
—GEORGE BUSH, AUGUST 3, 2005

SEVERAL SERENDIPITOUS EVENTS LINED UP FOR ME IN
early August 2005 that would allow the miraculous events of
Camp Casey to happen.

First of all, I was invited to Dallas during the first weekend
of August to be one of the keynote speakers at that year's Veterans For Peace convention. Many people think that I just fell
off the pumpkin truck in Crawford on August 6 and got involved in the antiwar movement, but readers of this book already know that I was deeply involved before then—so much
so that I was sought out by VFP to speak. Dallas is only about
two hours away from Crawford, so I just happened to be "in
the area."

After the Downing Street Memo hearings in June, I was invited, along with Congressman John Conyers and Ann Wright, to come to London to conduct Downing Street Memo hearings there. Col. Ann Wright was a twenty-nine-year member of the Army, in the Reserves, and an employee of the State Department who publicly resigned the day George Bush invaded Iraq. We were all set to go, and the group in England had even purchased a ticket for me, when Congressman Conyers had to call off the trip for some reason.

I had also been invited for a weeklong seminar in Arkansas, but the group there had decided to focus on other issues besides the war—so that trip was canceled, too. All of a sudden, I had the entire month of August free after the VFP convention. I was looking forward to a quiet month of swimming, sunning, looking for a place to live, and just trying to get my life in order.

Back on June 1, Pat had asked me to move out of the house so he could "get on with his life." I left and moved in with a friend in Berkeley, but that did not work out, so I moved back into our home in Vacaville and turned the back room into a little apartment for myself. I was living in the house with Andy, Janey, and Pat, but Pat and I rarely saw each other or had any contact. I would leave the house in the mornings, go to the gym and then to a local coffee shop to work on e-mails, strategies for protest, making travel arrangements for myself, etc., for the rest of the day. Once in a while, the kids would come to my "office" and eat lunch with me. I would usually go to one of the restaurants where the girls worked for dinner.

Then August 3 happened. That day I was doing two things that I didn't normally do. I was sitting at home by myself, and I was watching television. I had the channel switched to one of the news networks.

While watching the news, I learned that fourteen Marines had been killed in Iraq in one incident. All of the Marines were from a unit in Ohio that had lost another six Marines just a few days prior. I was devastated. I was stunned. I was heartbroken for the families and for the lives cut so cruelly short by Bush's lies. I was heartbroken for myself sitting in the living room surrounded by Casey's things and medals and awards and pictures and immersed in all of the lost dreams and lost opportunities and the future.

I began typing an e-mail to my address list of about three hundred people and I was feeling so sad and frustrated. I had been working so hard for so long and yet it seemed so little was being accomplished. I was frustrated that the media and Congress weren't doing their respective jobs and the American public was all but in a coma of denial and complacency.

In my e-mail I was expressing my sorrow for the Marines and their families and my frustration when George Bush came on my TV and said, "The families of the fallen can rest assured that their loved ones died for a noble cause," and that we here in America had to remain steadfast in our mission to honor "the sacrifices of the ones who have fallen."

I literally saw red and I was typing these exact words into my e-mail as I thought them:

"I am going to Dallas this weekend to speak at the Veterans For Peace convention. After I am finished, I am going down to Crawford, and I am going to drive up as far as I can go and I am going to demand to meet with that m.f.'er and I am going to ask him for what noble cause did he kill Casey and to demand that he stop using Casey's sacrifice to justify more killing."

I said that Dede would go with me. I hit the send button, and the rest is history.

I had to leave right away for a speaking engagement in Sacramento and on the way I made three calls. The first call was to Dede, to let her know what we were going to be doing that Saturday. Without hesitation, she said, "Okay!" The second call was to Andrea Buffa from CodePink Alert: Women for Peace and Global Exchange to ask her to send out a press release. CodePink and Global Exchange are two organizations that were founded by my friend Medea Benjamin. Andrea, Medea, and I worked together in Florida for about a week during the 2004 elections. Ever since that time, we've helped each other with our common goal of ending the war.

My third call went to Amy Branham, another Gold Star Mother and a member of our group who was going to meet us in Dallas to hang out with Dede and me during the convention. I told her my plans and invited her to go along with us, and without hesitation she agreed.

And that was how the most amazing and effective antiwar action of this current conflict started. I was accused many times of planning the Crawford action so far in advance and of being "used" as a "tool" of (insert name of your favorite lefty group, or traitorous moviemaker, here).

The Camp Casey Peace Movement started that quickly, that spontaneously, and that easily—but as I have said, it was a natural outgrowth of what I had already been doing up to then.

I will tell you more about the Crawford experience in the next chapter, but it was such an organic experience—we literally made it up as we went along. Did we make some mistakes? Hell, yes! But nothing had ever been done like Camp Casey up until then, and we were trying our hardest every day to be effective under some of the most difficult circumstances: the heat, the hate, the fire ants, the egos, etc. I think even with the mistakes, the event was highly successful and it remains successful, judging by the right-wing attacks that are still leveled at me every day.

When I returned from my speech at the Sacramento Democratic Club, I turned my computer on: I had about six hundred e-mails! It appeared that my original e-mail had gone around the country a few times. I had barely thought about what I had done in sending out that e-mail until I saw the response. That's when I knew that I had something here. The evening of August 3 was when I first suspected that going to Crawford was a good idea.

There were a few things that I hadn't even thought of until then. What would I do if George Bush met with me? (Even I, Mrs. Optimist, felt that probability was low.) What would I do if he didn't meet with me? At that point my entire scheme was to rent a car and drive to Crawford after I was finished with the meeting in Dallas.

The evening of August 3 was also the first time I had ever heard of the Crawford Peace House. I got an e-mail from Hadi Jawad, one of the directors, who would be accused of being a terrorist during Camp Casey that summer. Hadi told me that he would be in Dallas and he would like to meet with me to talk about the "action" and how the Crawford Peace House could support me in what I was doing. Hadi was also scheduled to speak at the same workshop where I was speaking during the convention.

A Crawford Peace House? What a fabulous idea, I remember thinking at the time. Why hadn't I ever heard of the Peace House and their work before? I wondered. Well, I was about to be intimately connected with the work of the Peace House and will forever be connected with the marvelous people who founded it and who continue to work for peace there.

Apparently my e-mail also went out to hundreds of VFP members, and I wasn't surprised at the vociferous support expressed in many of the e-mails I received. I was surprised, however, by the ones that accused me of trying to sabotage the convention by my actions—I tried to reassure the VFP (and some of their rather unreassurable members) that I wasn't trying to sabotage their convention—I was honestly unprepared to find that some previously supportive people seemed to be turning against me and what I thought was a necessary step in ending the war!

I left for Dallas the next day. I had packed—just for the weekend—and I drove my car down to Los Angeles to hook up with Dede and we flew from there. When I locked my car in front of my sister's mobile home, little did I know that it would remain there for over a month! When I kissed my kids good-bye, little did I know that I wouldn't see them again for over a month, and that that month—even that one day, August 6—was going to turn our lives upside down. Little did I know that I was leaving Vacaville, as my home, for the last time, never to return. Little did I know that when I drove out of Vacaville, I was driving from relative obscurity to almost overnight, international notoriety—with all the perks and pains that entailed.

If I had known all of that, would I still have done what I did on August 6? The answer to that question is an emphatic Yes!!!

When I arrived in Dallas, the convention's welcoming dinner was in full swing and many of the Vets were already "in their cups." I got lots of hugs and love, but also some warnings about not "screwing up the convention" with my action on Saturday.

The president of the VFP straight out told me that Saturday was the business part of the convention, when the goals of the entire next year were to be decided. There was already talk of a mass mutiny on Saturday because all of the vets wanted to come to Crawford with me. It seems the "business" part was not the most popular or well-attended part of the convention anyway. I kept telling all of the vets, over and over again, that I never asked for their support or their accompaniment. They were all grown men and women and if they wanted to come with me, they could, and if they didn't want to come with me, they didn't have to. I love them all, but I refused to get in the middle of a "big baby" fest.

On the Friday before we went down to Crawford, we had a meeting to plan the action. That meeting was attended by myself, Dede, Hadi, Hadi's partner Valley, Mike McPherson of the VFP, and Lisa Fithian, an Austin-based activist.

The first question for me came from Hadi. He asked me what I was going to do if the president didn't meet with me. I answered him with the first words that popped into my mind: "I am not leaving Crawford until he meets with me, or until his vacation is over. I am going to sit down and refuse to move."

Whoa! We all looked at each other stunned, because I even surprised myself with this. I will never forget for the rest of my life what Hadi said, reverently breaking the silence: "Wow, that's an action." One by one, the people at the historic meeting agreed with Hadi. He was right: that was an action!

The rest of the meeting is a blur to me. There was talk about logistics, tents, water, permits, other activists who had tried to cross the Secret Service line in Crawford, blah, blah, blah—I was not concerned with the logistics, or planning, I was just eager to go and confront the president on his vacation.

One of the e-mails that I received after I sent out the auspicious one on August 3 was from one of my former friends in Vacaville. She had never supported what I was doing in trying to expose the lies of George Bush, and I wasn't buying her sickly sweet e-mail this time. She wrote to me, "Cindy, if you didn't use such harsh language, maybe you would reach more people who are sitting on the fence!" I responded with the same words I used at the VFP convention that Friday night:

"How in the world is anybody sitting on that fence? If you fall on the side that is pro-George and pro-war, then get your ass over to Iraq and take the place of someone who wants to come home. And if you fall on the side that is against this war and against George Bush, stand up and speak out. But whatever side you fall on, quit being on the fence."

I still believe this. I still believe that there are many, many chickenhawks in this country who cheerlead for a war that never should have been fought, who themselves avoided Vietnam like the plague but who want *my* son to fight and die. And for what? To feed their macho, testosterone-laden egos and to avenge the horrible drubbing our country took in Vietnam? To shoot their pent-up wads in a war that they thought was going to be a "cakewalk" but which has proven to be whatever is the opposite of a cakewalk—a pie throw? If the reasons for the invasion weren't bad enough, what about the way these armchair-cowardly warriors have fucked everything up from the get-go?

I think we have to ask ourselves two questions about anyone who still supports the continued cluster-fuck in Iraq: What is he/she gaining monetarily or politically? And what media outlets does he/she get their propaganda from?

That Friday night after my speech, I was exhausted, but I had two interviews to do on late-night radio. One was with my friend Mike Malloy from Air America, who was worried about me but very supportive of what I was about to do. I was exhausted but I couldn't sleep. I wouldn't let on to anyone, but I was terrified of going to Crawford.

I was terrified to further expose myself and my grief. The further along I go in my grieving process, the more I know how much it hurts to put my sorrow out to a public where there is a segment of the population that wants to take my grief and turn it into something ugly. How can anyone question a mother-in-mourning's motives, when all she is doing is trying to save other mothers from the same gut-wrenching experience? How can anybody in the twenty-first century still be in favor of killing innocent people to solve problems?

I knew when I went down that road in Crawford, no matter how many VFPers, GSFPers, IVAWers, MFSOers, CodePinkers, or any other concerned citizens were with me, I would be alone. I would be as alone in this as I was every time I gave birth, or when I fell on the floor in my cosmic grief heap on 04/04/04. I was alone that day and I am still alone. No matter how many people support me and my work, I am alone.

I also knew that when I marched down that lonely road, I would be the focus of the right-wing hate machine. I already knew how vicious they could be from my Downing Street days. I knew that this time they would show no mercy. I knew, and the death threats that I received confirmed the fact, that it was going to be my ass on the line—literally and figuratively.

After I lay down in my twin bed in the University of Dallas dorm room that I shared with Dede on that steamy hot Texas night (by now early morning, August 6), I got a phone call from my daughter Janey. She was upset because I had put some of my clothes in her closet. Pat had been nagging me for weeks to get my clothes out of his closet, but I didn't know where to put them. No matter how much I told her that I was sorry and I wouldn't have done it if I knew it would upset her so much, she kept attacking me about it.

I finally said, "Janey, it's not the clothes. Why have you called me this late? What is really the matter?" She told me that she wanted me to be home more and be her real mother again. I felt so alone.

After much debate and hurt feelings, it was decided that twelve people from the VFP convention would accompany me to Crawford. Four guys from VFP, four guys from IVAW (Iraq Veterans Against the War), and four guys from VVAW (Vietnam Veterans Against the War). They were going to drive Gold Star Mother Amy Branham and me to Crawford in the so-called Impeachment Tour bus. This bus had been driven from Northern California by Patrick and Gordon, two members of a local VFP chapter. They bought the bus and painted it and named it the Impeachment Tour bus. Dede would follow us in the car that we had rented in Dallas.

After some picture taking and speech making and name calling (from the small contingent that were vehemently opposed to even the twelve going), we were off. There were already about twenty cars behind us on the trek from Dallas to Crawford. This little "parade" from Dallas to Crawford was made up of members of CodePink as well as ordinary citizens from around Texas, and a few from other parts of the country who wanted to join us that day. They lined up behind the bus and away we went.

There were some dear friends of mine on the bus: Camilo Mejia, who is a conscientious objector from this Iraq war, and Dennis Kyne, a veteran of the first conflict in the gulf who has done some amazing work advocating for vets who suffer from depleted-uranium sickness. I also made some new friends, including Patrick and Gordon who drove the bus, and Billy Kelly. Billy is an amazing man who has friends all over the world. One of my newest but dearest friends, Daniel Ellsberg, the man who famously leaked the Pentagon Papers to *The New York Times* in 1971, went to school with Billy Kelly. We were having fun on the bus, but partway through the three-hour bus ride in the raging Texas heat I got a horrible headache and went to lie down on one of the back bunks for a while.

Dede called me at one point during the very beginning of the ride to Crawford, and she was crying. She confessed that she had also been scared out of her mind, but the first song she heard when she turned on the car radio was "Whip It" by Devo. That song was popular when Casey was about two and he used to dance around and sing to it: "Whip it. Whip it dood."

But the song goes: "When a problem comes along, you must whip it!" Well, we were heading to Crawford to "whip" the problem.

When Dede called to tell me about the song, it reminded

me of when I was so torn about leaving Pat. I went up to Casey's park to sit by him and talk to him about it. I was journaling and trying to listen to my son to try to do the right thing. I got up to leave, got in my car, turned on the radio, and after about a split-second pause in the airwaves, Casey's absolute favorite all-time song, from his absolute favorite all-time band, came on: "Jump" by Van Halen. I took that as a sign to jump out of my twenty-eight-year marriage. By that time, I had learned to believe the old saying, "There is no such thing as coincidence."

We eventually arrived at the Crawford Peace House and were joined by another twenty or so cars, and then we prepared to convoy up as close to the ranch as the county sheriff would let us. I was getting impatient, though, because he was taking so long to let us go. I had no idea why we had to wait in the hot bus for such a long time before we got under way. Was it to warn other law enforcement, Secret Service, or whoever that so many of us were coming? Was it to quell the already growing media frenzy? Was it our first taste of the government machine trying to discourage us? I don't know, but none of it worked.

When we finally got to the now famous triangle that would become Camp Casey, there were about seventy-five media people waiting there. We disembarked from the bus and gathered at one of the points of the triangle to hold a press conference. I was hot and tired from the ride but impatient to begin the walk to the president's ranch. I held up a picture of baby Casey and I said that we were marching up to George Bush's ranch to confront him about the lies that led to Casey's death and to Amy's son Jeremy's death. With Amy, Dede, and me in the lead, we headed down the road, with the sheriff warning us all to stay in the ditch. He said if we went on the public road, we would have to stop. This despite the fact that the sheriff had blocked off the roads to traffic.

God, it was so hot that day. I think it was the hottest day of the entire month, except for the last Saturday. The sun was beating down upon us. About seventy-five of us began our walk for peace and our entry into the annals of history (and histrionics) that day. I forget what we were chanting, but it is all recorded on DVD somewhere.

My friend Dennis Kyne told me that I could come out of the snake-infested ditch and walk on the road because we always got at least one warning before "the man" clamped down. So I, in my immature babyhood state of activism, got on the road, but barely, just enough to not be in the ditch. All of a sudden, a police cruiser barreled past us and blocked the road to prevent any further progress.

I went up to the car and the sherriffs said that we had broken the rules by walking on the road. I begged them to not be tools of the government. I begged them to not be the ones to stop us from our mission. I begged them to take a message to the president, but they wouldn't budge, so I just sat down in the ditch by the side of the road.

I sat down with the picture of my darling baby boy Casey. I sat in the hot Texas sun and proclaimed to the world that I wasn't moving until George Bush came out to meet with me.

Please understand, I didn't want to stay there. I wanted to go home and be a real mother to Janey. I didn't want to sit in the blistering heat. I wanted to go back to the Peace House and rest in the air-conditioned space there. I didn't want to spend August in Crawford. I wanted to spend it in Vacaville, swimming, sunning, and resting up for the busy actions in the fall. I didn't want to do any of it, but I did it anyway, because I had to.

Sitting with me at first was Diane Wilson, a member of CodePink and an environmental activist from the Houston area. She vowed to stay with me. Amy and Dede went back to the Peace House for water but then were denied entry back to where Diane and I were sitting down, so we went back to the triangular area to get water, and where there was some shade. We decided that this spot would be our camp until George met with us, or until his vacation was finished at the end of August.

We were sitting in the shade trying to cool down when we decided that our camp, like all proper camps, needed a name. These are some of the ideas we had: Camp Truth. Camp Freedom. Camp Peace. Then my dear sweet adopted son, Camilo Mejia, said, "Camp Casey." Again, we all looked at each other with reverence, because we all knew that was the name of our camp. I cried, of course. What a gift Casey had given us—to all be together, gathered in his name for peace!

We dedicated the area in Casey's name to all of the men and women who had their futures robbed from them by this insane war that so many of us already opposed. We dedicated Camp Casey to peace: to ensure that our fallen heroes would have died for peace and love; not violence and hatred. We were there to ask one question: "For what noble cause?" But we all already knew for what noble cause we came to Crawford that miserably hot August day: peace. Peace, peace, peace.

The VFPers had to get back to Dallas to finish the rest of their weekend, and most of the other marchers left to go wherever they had to go, promising one by one as they left to return at some point during the vigil—no matter how long it lasted. Now there were just seven of us who would stay there throughout the dark, lonely night.

While we were sitting there wondering what we should do next, about four white SUVs came barreling up the road and skidded to a halt in front of us and soon we were surrounded by Secret Service agents. "Does he want to speak to me now?" I called out. One agent laughed openly when I said that.

Two men dressed in very casual clothes came up to my lawn chair. One introduced himself as Joe Hagin, deputy chief of staff to George, and the other as Stephen Hadley, national security adviser to George. Joe plopped down in a lawn chair next to me, and Steve sat on the ground. We offered them water, which they declined.

Steve asked me what I wanted to tell the president and I told him, although I am sure he already knew. Joe and Steve then tried to ply me with the usual propaganda about WMD and the war on terror, etc.

I finally had enough of their bullshit and I said, "Just because I am a grieving mother, do not make the mistake of thinking that I am a stupid grieving mother. I am very well informed, and I don't think you even believe the crap you are telling me."

Steve actually looked a little embarrassed and said, "We don't think you are stupid. We didn't come down here to change your mind on policy."

I said, "Yes, you did. That's exactly what you thought. You thought I would be so impressed by your titles and your convincing arguments that I would leave. Well, I'm not, and I am not going to leave. You're wasting your time. The next person I want to speak to from up there is your boss."

They said good-bye and hopped back into their SUVs and sped away.

The two things that were funny about that meeting were that the same agent that cracked up when I first asked if George wanted to meet with me kept making faces behind Joe and Steve's backs, mimicking them while they were talking, almost causing me to lose my composure a couple of times. And when Joe and Steve were spilling some bullshit beans on me, I said, "Do you guys stop and think sometimes, 'Wow, I really work for an idiot?' " Both of their eyes sparkled at that one, and I could tell they actually wanted to laugh. But they were both so fake-concerned and serious, they couldn't let it out. I wasn't impressed.

There was also a Secret Service agent who kept coming and telling us that if we stayed the night there, we would probably be run over by a speeding car in the night. We finally asked him why he was so sure about that. Would it be the SS that ran us over? We got it out to the blogosphere that if we died, we would probably have been murdered by the SS—so that near catastrophe was averted! I never again saw that SS agent who had appeared to be so concerned for our safety that first day. He was handsome, though. I did ask him how he could protect and possibly die for a man that was so loathsome and all he said was, "It's my job."

There were just a few of us left to spend the lonely Crawford night together: myself, Diane, Dede, Amy, Desiree and Hillary (two members of CodePink), and a man named Jim, our guardian angel. Just like an angel sent to watch over us, when we didn't need protection anymore, he faded away. Jim was such an indispensable part of that first night. He was calm, cool, collected, and his presence comforted the rest of us.

After I recovered at the Peace House for a few hours from what some medics from Iraq diagnosed later as "heat exhaustion," I returned to the triangle. It was pitch-black! The seven of us had a lawn chair each, one flashlight, and a bucket to relieve ourselves in. It was a spooky but wonderful night. In some ways, I think it was the best night of the vigil.

We sat around all night worried about being run over, looking at the stars, talking, marveling, just being together.

We had received word that people were lighting candles and putting them in their windows all over the world in solidarity with us. My phone was ringing off the hook with messages of support. We couldn't help but feel small under the vast sky above us, but also protected and gratified by all the support we were generating.

We were awake all night together, that first night. Then Dede had to pull out early the next morning to get back to California and to work, and Amy left early for Houston. Hillary and Desiree left, only to come back many times. Jim, our angel, also left after more support came from the VFP convention. And that left Diane and me alone there for just a few hours. That night was the most peaceful and magical night of the entire month. If we had known the chaos that would ensue, I am sure we would have savored it and each other even more.

Then, slowly but surely, the people started coming, building up to more than fifteen thousand by the time the vigil ended on August 31. That is a separate chapter, though.

It was like I said at the triangle after it was christened Camp Casey:

This is the beginning of the end of the occupation of Iraq.

Thus began the peaceful occupation of Crawford.

Chapter 10

Camp Casey

"I had to come, I don't even know why."
—CAMP CASEY VISITOR, AUGUST 2005

AS THE SECOND ANNIVERSARY OF CASEY'S DEATH IN Iraq has just passed, I am frequently asked by the media what is the worst thing and what is the best thing that I have experienced since his death. Well, Casey's death is the worst thing that I have ever experienced in my entire life. Anything "bad" that has happened next to that doesn't compare, come close, or even approach the same universe as Casey dying. If there is something that is worse than that, I don't even want to know about it.

The best thing, by far, is the Camp Casey experience. With all of the already mentioned "difficulties," Republicans, Karl Rove and the smear machine, Camp Casey was still the most amazing and miraculous thing that has ever happened to me.

I look back on the twenty-six days of Camp Casey as some of the most stressful days of my life (subtracting every day in terms of Casey's death), but strangely, I also look back on those days as the best days of my life.

There was plenty of heartache, stress, upset, drama, sorrow, and even rage to go around, but on the flip (and better) side of the coin, there was laughter, love, joy, and, best of all, hope. Hope is the overriding emotion of Camp Casey, and it is the expression of hope and the regaining of my hope that I will be grateful for for the rest of my life. It was losing hope when I lost Casey that I now know fueled my thoughts of suicide. The salvaging of my hope was what kept me going through those twenty-six days of work and worry. I thought my hope was dead, but it was miraculously resurrected during August of 2005.

The most ironic aspect of Camp Casey was that it wouldn't have happened at all if George had met with me that first day. George was the reason my hope almost evaporated to nothing, and George was also the reason that I recovered my hope. There are days where I don't know whether to send him chocolates or an exploding Cuban cigar. I think I should share all my honors with him. George is the one who really sparked the peace movement by his thoughtless and imprudent inaction in August. If he had met with me on the first day it would have defused everything. If he had met with me any other day in August, we would have left. He didn't, so here we are.

The reason coming to Camp Casey gave everyone else so much hope is that for almost five years of the Bush regime and living under a virtual dictatorship of one-party rule, we felt as if we were losing our country. Many of us felt that there was nothing we could do to stem the tide of creeping fascism and out-of-control government. We were frustrated because we had seemingly done everything that we could to defeat Bush, but like a movie vampire or the Terminator, he refused to stay defeated. I know that I and a majority of the others who came to Camp Casey were at the end of our ropes.

I and many other peace activists tried and tried to think of something big to do to call attention to the fact that BushCo was waging such a lawless and brutal war of aggression in Iraq. I remembered the horrible self-immolations of the Buddhist monks during Vietnam, and I prayed that it would not come to that. But, even without being able to come up with a plan, I knew I would be figuratively immolated by the hate-journalists for whatever I did. Like I said, I was willing to take that kind of risk.

Hallelujah for Camp Casey! We didn't have to immolate ourselves, we just had to endure twenty-six days of heat, fire ants, thunder-and-lightning storms, and constant attacks to bring our cause to the attention of mainstream America, and people were paying attention. That is why we got our hope back. That is why we were so filled with joy! We finally remembered something that we had forgotten after so many years of tyranny and oppression: We the people of the United States of America have the power. Our governments govern only with the permission of the people.

Before I get into some of the little-known facts and anecdotes about Camp Casey, I need to recount some of the miracles that have happened since August of 2005.

John Murtha (D-Pa.) came out of the war closet and said that the war is a mistake and our troops need to come home within six months. He should know: He is a former Iraq war supporter and decorated Vietnam vet who shook with sorrow when he called for the end to the war. He was attacked by the righties, who even tried to question his motives in going to military hospitals such as Walter Reed in D.C. to visit the wounded soldiers. He even helped their families with money if they needed it. The righties questioned his motives and scrutinized his tax returns. Scotty McClellan, the moon-faced and deceptively honest-looking White House spokesperson, even compared Congressman Murtha to Michael Moore. Being compared to Michael Moore is an honor to me, and Michael was rightfully indignant about the entire episode, but now if one is on the correct side of the war issue and tells the truth about it, according to our government, you are automatically with the likes of Michael Moore! Gadzooks!

As of this writing, support for the war and support for George Bush has dwindled into the low thirties percentagewise in this country. BushCo and the right-wingers are busy trying, but failing, to shore up support for their war crimes . . . and speaking of war crimes, people are now starting to talk of Iraq in those terms, which *never* happened before Camp Casey. People are also talking about impeachment, which was, apparently, crazy talk when I wrote my open letter to George on November 4, 2004.

Concerned citizens all over the country set up semipermanent Camp Caseys and confronted their House reps and senators, advocating an end to the occupation and getting arrested and otherwise putting their comfort second and their country first. Contrary to weak MSM (mainstream media) reporting, more than five hundred thousand citizens came to Washington, D.C., on September 24, 2005. Many of them told me it was their first-ever protest, and they were there because of Camp Casey.

When I am called a "nutcase" or far-left radical, I remind people that more than two-thirds of this country believes the same way I do now, and more than 90 percent of the human race believes that this war is wrong and the coalition troops should leave Iraq ASAP. I am not a nutcase or radical militant war protestor, I am mainstream America. Two-thirds of the country crosses all demographic lines: right, left; rich, poor; black, white; old, young; believer, atheist; gay, straight: whichever way we would like to divide ourselves, most of us want the madness in the Middle East to be over.

A challenge for the antiwar movement, which I prefer to call the peace movement, is now to figure out a way to mobilize the vast majority of Americans who want the war to end. I believe we have defined the problem and convinced as many people as we are going to convince that this war is wrong and that George Bush and the rest of the neocons are criminals. Now how do we translate this into action to bring the troops home? Not only do we have to convince them to act, but we have to convince everyone that each and every American has a stake in what is going on in Iraq. That every minute we allow the killing to continue is another stain on our humanity. Every dollar dumped into the sands of Iraq is another dollar not spent here in America in our communities: billions and billions of dollars that will have to be absorbed and paid back by our descendants. I do not want that burden on my heart!

The first full day I spent at Camp Casey was Sunday, August 7. We housed about two dozen people that night. All of the people there were friends of mine or fellow activists who quickly became friends. Sunday was a horrible day. My daughters left for Europe without me being there to say good-bye; people were calling me on my phone and calling me a "traitor," "un-American," "deranged," "communist," etc.

I was answering my phone and doing interview upon interview. The biggest "controversy" that arose that day was the idea that I had already met with George Bush once, so why did I think I deserved another meeting? I will answer this question for you, just as I answered all of the reporters: When I met with him in June of 2004, I was a different person. I was still in shock and denial about my son's death.

When Casey marched off to this illegal and immoral war, I vaguely knew that the war was wrong. I suspected that George Bush and the rest of his cabal were lying, but I didn't know for sure. After Casey was killed, a raft of convincing proofs emerged: the 9/11 Commission reports dispelled the lies that Saddam had anything to do with the terrible tragedy in New York City; the Senate Intelligence report (the first half at least, which is the only part that has been published) also dispelled this; the WMD report commissioned by BushCo proved that Saddam had no WMD, or even any hope of acquiring WMD for over a decade; and most damning of all to me, the Downing Street Memos indicating that the Bush regime was planning on invading Iraq no matter what, and the intelligence had to be "fixed around the policy." I was pissed. Casey should still be alive. No one else should be dying!

I was lying in my tent that second night, on a blow-up mattress, feeling as alone as anyone could ever possibly feel. I was second-guessing myself and wondering what the hell I had started. What had I gotten myself and about a dozen other people into? I reassured my very upset and tired self that I had only twenty-four days left. I could handle anything for twenty-four days, and if it brought our young people home from Iraq even one day sooner, I could take it! I knew I could take anything that was thrown at me by the crazies, the administration, Karl Rove, Rush Limbaugh, Bill O'Reilly, anyone. I knew I could do it. I would treat the experience like a youth group campout and we would endure the month.

Going from enduring the days and counting them down to when I *could* leave Crawford to counting the days down when I *had* to leave was the most amazing transformation to me that August. It took me only five days to get over the feeling that I had to endure Camp Casey to experience feelings of gratitude for being there.

On Thursday of the first week, more than seven hundred people came out to Camp Casey from all over. A middle-aged, well-dressed couple came up to me and said that they'd come all the way from Wisconsin to hug me! I asked them how long they were staying. The man replied that they just came to hug me and they had to drive back to Wisconsin right away because they had to go to work the next day!

Another couple who came to Camp Casey were on their way from California to Florida for a vacation. They heard about Camp Casey and came to Crawford to spend their vacation there instead. The man was an artist who did pencil drawings of everyone. Many hundreds of Americans—ranging from aging "hippies" who had protested the Vietnam War to entire families with babies, young children, and teens—changed their vacation plans to come to Crawford.

When we first sat in the ditches on August 6, we were inhabiting what would become known as Camp Casey I. We set up tents and awnings and the crosses from the VFP exhibit, Arlington West, along two sides of the triangle. We couldn't camp or park in the triangle itself anymore, because, mysteriously, on about the fourth or fifth day, the sheriffs came out and said the neighbor across from the third side of the triangle "remembered" that she owned the triangle and kicked us off.

Subsequent investigative reporting showed that there was never a transfer from the county to the neighbor who evicted us from the triangle. I don't care what anybody says, though, I can't believe that the sheriff's department of the county where the president of the United States lives has even an infinitesimal doubt about who owns any property on the road that the prez passes along. I never bought the bullshit that they finally "discovered" that the county didn't own the land. The sheriffs showed up one day and said that they would confiscate any car or tent that was left on the land—immediately. When we ended Camp Casey, we left as good friends of the law enforcement agencies there, but I still believe that the whole land question was really shady and exigent.

One day I was along the side of a road, filming a commercial asking for George to meet with me, when a neighbor lady came home and almost ran us over. She told us she would kill us if we didn't get off her property, when in fact we were on an easement.

Then there was Mr. Mattlage across the road, who shot his rifle off during a prayer service that we were conducting. In Texas, shooting is fine as long as it is done on one's own property. He claimed to be shooting at "doves."

But the evening when another local Bubba ran over our crosses, destroying over one hundred of them, was the most egregious example of redneck ignorance that we witnessed during our vigil. He was caught minutes after he vandalized our camp and dishonored our fallen heroes because one of the crosses got stuck in his wheel well, popping his tire.

Another hypocrite for killing! We in the peace movement

are always accused of not supporting our troops, or of spitting on the graves of our children if we don't support the evil mission and the scandalous commander in chief. Then Bubba comes, with his truck dragging chains and a pipe, and mows down the crosses that we had set up to honor our children. Another cowardly, hypocritical warnik! The Bubbas of the world, whether they drive trucks in Crawford or hide in bulletproof limos in D.C., are despicable and beneath notice, or would be if they weren't so atrociously destructive!

After Bubba Mattlage fired his shotgun at us and after we were threatened with eviction from Camp Casey, I was sitting in the Peace House working on my blog when a tall, self-effacing man walked in. His name was Fred Mattlage and he was Bubba Mattlage's third cousin. He was appalled at what Bubba and the rest of the neighbors were doing, so he offered us two acres of land closer to George's ranch—that is the land that became Camp Casey II. The offer—coming just when we were despairing of having a place to conduct our vigil and fearing the dangerous neighbors—was another miraculous occurrence. It was like the times when we would be running out of something important, such as ice, and an unbidden ice truck would roll up and make a large donation. Or the time after the Bubba ran over our crosses and the next day thirty-five dozen roses were piled on my lap by a man in a delivery truck! Miracles like this occurred every day.

Fred Mattlage was inundated with notes of thanks from all over the progressive, peace-loving world. His was a kind and generous gesture made out of anger at his cousin, but also out of shame for the way Crawford was treating us. He wanted to let us know, and he did overwhelmingly, that not everyone in Crawford was a Bubba! We already knew by the hundreds of people who came from all over the state that George the Carpetbagger was not universally loved in Texas.

I realize that having hundreds, sometimes thousands of people move into your neighborhood virtually overnight must be difficult, but we were good and peaceful neighbors. Also, the reason that we were there was to confront the king in his castle. People of all stripes were suffering horribly from the occupation in Iraq, and I thought that our neighbors in Texas could stand us for a few weeks. We were only a semipermanent camp.

Our little camp was bursting at its seams. Where would we put the hundreds of Americans who continued to come out to show their support for us? We felt we were in hostile territory and we were worried about people being hurt by cars that were constantly coming down the prairie road.

The day that we were scheduled to move to Camp II, we got the devastating news from California that my mom had suffered a stroke. Dede, who was back in camp at the time, and I were on a plane to California within two hours of getting the news.

When we got to the tiny airport in Waco, the national press corps was waiting for us and they watched Dede and me board the plane. Upon our arrival in Dallas to await our plane to Los

Angeles, not only was Amy Goodman from *Democracy Now!* and her crew there waiting for us, I was greeted by pilots and passengers who wanted to tell me that my mom was in their prayers! Everyone had already heard about it. My girls, Carly and Janey, who were in Italy at the time, heard it on the news there! Pat and I had decided not to tell them while they were on vacation, and they were steaming mad at us for that!

Joan Baez traveled to Camp Casey and arrived there the Saturday after I left for Los Angeles to be with my mom. Ironically, we were having a "mother's day" at Camp Casey and we were hosting mothers from all over the country who had gathered to write to Laura Bush demanding that she talk to her husband about bringing the troops home. We were scheduled to march to the checkpoint of the ranch and deliver the letters, but Dede and I ended up leaving before then.

Joan came out and kept the peace "troops" rallied while I was gone. When I returned, she and I got really close. One morning, I was sitting in my bedroom in my trailer talking to a friend on the phone, when Joan walked in wearing my bra on her head! I burst out in laughter and I told my friend, "Oh, my God! Joan Baez just walked in my room with my bra on her head!" If someone had asked me the least likely sentence I would ever utter, I would have to pick that one.

Another amazing moment came on August 28, the final Sunday at Camp Casey: Martin Sheen came to recite a rosary with me and for the camp. I had been asked to do a photo shoot for Oprah's magazine before the rosary started. I was in my trailer getting makeup done by a professional makeup artist, and I was chatting with Martin, who came bearing gifts, including a prop that had been on his desk for the entire time he was on *The West Wing:* a plaque that had a quote from John Kennedy on it. He also gave me his personal rosary, which I carry with me everywhere I go.

On that particular Sunday afternoon, I was feeling a little tired and puckish because the night before, Tiffany, Alicia, myself, some IVAW young men, and Randi Rhodes, a talk-show host on Air America Radio, gathered at the bed-and-breakfast that Jodie Evans, cofounder of CodePink, had rented for the month of August in Crawford, and we had ourselves a little party! It was the first but certainly not the last time Randi, who has become a dear friend of mine, and I drank together. Somehow, when I am with Randi, it always involves a mild hangover the next day!

Everyone who came out to Camp Casey, somehow or another, evolved into doing certain jobs. Erik Lobo came out from Chicago and was involved in setting up our infirmary at Camp Casey II. Barbara Cummings came from San Diego and became what we called our "Parking Nazi," directing shuttles to and from the Peace House to Camp Casey. Barbara has also become a great friend of mine and an amazing supporter of progressive causes.

Gerry Fonseca came from Slidell, Louisiana, while I was away in Los Angeles and became my personal security agent after I returned. Gerry was never far away from me, and he always made sure I had an ice-cold water in my hand. He rarely slept and, I found out later, would guard my trailer while I was "sleeping." Gerry was also one of the people whose life was turned upside down during Hurricane Katrina. He lost everything, but he stayed at Camp Casey for the last few days anyway. So many people came out and put their entire hearts and souls into making Camp Casey such an enormous success.

The last Sunday at Camp Casey two couples got married: one couple at Camp I and one couple at Camp II. Peter and Genevieve were from Austin, and they had been working at Camp Casey II when I was gone taking care of my mom. When I returned from California, they asked permission to have their wedding at Camp Casey. They said that they had never been in a place so full of love and they wanted to begin their married life there.

While I was gone taking care of my mom, a certain GSFP member came to Crawford, apparently to try to wrest control of Camp Casey from me. We were in the process of opening Camp II before I left, and this Gold Star brother was trying to make all kinds of changes, even calling it "Camp Gold Star." A few people who had been at Camp Casey from the beginning even left because this person was using heavy-handed, almost dictatorial tactics. Some of my Camp Casey friends were calling me in tears because of his behavior. I finally called the GSFP brother and told him that we didn't use draconian measures at Camp Casey. Camp Casey was a place of love and hope, and Camp II was Camp Casey II—not Camp Gold Star. I was furious that his unloving attitude chased away some very loyal volunteers.

He and his mother and another Gold Star mom had visited Camp Casey before and even then had made my life a freaking stressful nightmare. I was surprised to discover that some of the MFSO members and GSFP members felt that people who hadn't experienced our personal losses didn't deserve to come out to Camp Casey, that they couldn't possibly share our deep and profound reaction to the war. They encouraged me not to allow fellow American peace activists to come to Camp Casey. I nixed that idea. I realized that the peace movement is a people's movement that can be led by our organization but can never be effective with only our participation. I was and still am astounded and thrilled that there are so many people who live here in our damaged country who know that everyone has a stake in this war, not just us. Everyone is harmed by the continuing occupation.

This mother/brother combo had been very close friends of mine up until Crawford. I frequently stayed at their family home when I was on the road and I really felt that they were part of my family and I was part of theirs. My entire family knew and loved their entire family, and when I heard that they would be there on Wednesday of the first week I was delighted. I had enough interviews and work to do for a hundred Gold Star Family members, and in fact our group was begging, and paying, for our members to be there. We even paid Ma/Bro's way.

I was sitting in the ditch, trying to stay cool, the afternoon that they first appeared. (If this were a movie instead of a book, ominous music would now begin playing.) I was intensely hot and immensely stressed: again, interview after interview—the media had even been out to watch me get my hair cut by a volunteer who brought the tools of her trade down from Austin. Boy, that was a slow news day!

Ma/Bro drove up in an air-conditioned car driven by a Camp Casey volunteer who had picked them up at the Waco airport. They were wearing nice travel clothes, still looking fresh, Ma was all made-up and Bro was snazzy in his silk shirt and chinos. I was in my Camp Casey uniform of shorts and sweaty and stinking T-shirt, no makeup—what was the use when it would melt off about ten minutes after I put it on?—and whatever sticky hat I could lay my hands on and plop on my head to protect my already deeply tanned face from more sun.

As soon as I saw Ma/Bro, I yelled with joy and ran up to them and threw my arms around them weeping in relief and gratitude. I needed the help, especially to welcome newcomers to Camp Casey. Ma and Bro gave me the warmest hugs, and I believed everything was hunky-dory. A staff person from Military Families Speak Out was also with Ma/Bro, someone with whom I had worked well in the past.

Well, little did I know that everything was not so hunky-dory in Ma/Bro land. They had come down to Crawford for a little piece of the control pie, and they had been there for no more than ten minutes when the attacks began.

I was on the phone doing a "phoner" with yet another radio show when Ma came up to me and crooked her finger in the come-here signal. I smiled and held up my index finger indicating that I would be there in a minute.

She didn't smile back, and she said, "No, come here now, Cindy." I grimaced at her, pointed at the phone, and indicated again that I would be with her in a sec.

Ma twirled around and stomped off. I thought, *Uh-oh—what the freak is wrong with her?* I knew I was about to get in trouble for something.

When I was finished with my interview I found Ma/Bro stewing down the road with the MFSO staff member. As soon as I walked up they attacked me. The biggest problem they had was the pink sign that said CAMP CASEY. They were really upset that the camp was named after Casey, and they were upset because it was pink. They had issues with the group CodePink—which I don't understand at all. CodePink has been and is one of the most effective direct-action, anti–Iraq war groups in the world right now. Ma/Bro didn't care that the IVAW members had named the camp after Casey. By the time they finally arrived in Crawford, though, it was already Camp Casey, and no one who was there wanted the name changed.

Another Gold Star mom who came out soon after Ma/Bro also insisted that I change the name, but the name stayed. Casey's mom started the action. Casey was honored by his brother and sister soldiers the first day. It's just the way things worked out. That day, Ma/Bro and MFSO reamed me for starting up the best antiwar action ever. I couldn't believe that I had eagerly anticipated their arrival.

My darling friend Jodie came to my rescue, and I hopped in my friend Johnny Wolf's truck and headed down to the Peace House with him to escape my good friends Ma/Bro.

When I think of friends made during Camp Casey and friends lost, I think of Jodie and Johnny and of Ma/Bro. I had met Jodie Evans before August 2005, but I didn't really know her. The third day that I was at Camp Casey, I got trapped at the Crawford Peace House all by myself. I was on the phone constantly doing interviews and I would hear five or six other interviewers call in and go to voice mail while I was talking. I had to be at the Peace House to plug in my phone. I was literally on the office floor bent over a yellow pad trying in vain to listen to my voice messages while my phone wouldn't stop ringing. (I will never put my personal phone number on another press release!) The Crawford Peace House is directly next to the railroad tracks and that entire morning while I was trapped doing interviews, I could hear the trains going by. I was seriously thinking of hopping on a moving train and pulling an "Agatha Christie" and just disappearing. It was all I could do to make myself stay there with what seemed like the entire free world on my case—for better or worse.

Just when I was getting ready to flush my phone down the only toilet we had at that point, I felt a tap on my shoulder—I almost jumped out of my hot, clammy skin because I thought I was alone. I looked up and there in all of her calm and sweet "pinkness" was Jodie. She had brought two CodePink "girls" with her: Tiffany Burns and Alicia Sexton, who would become my closest assistants, confidantes, gofers, present holders, water fetchers, buffers, and all-around friends. Tiffany and Alicia are themselves best friends from high school, and I don't know what I would have done without them.

Jodie was something else. From the moment she got to Crawford, when she took the yellow pad and phone away from me and made me go to the bathroom, eat, drink, and rest a second while the girls very ably managed the voice mail and incoming calls, Jodie became my darling friend, supporter, and helper. Jodie is a tallish, stunning redhead with a pale complexion and knockout figure. She would be the last person you would think could endure twenty-six days of the Crawford heat and stress. But not only did she endure, she thrived and worked late into every night, well after she had made me go to bed (I would grudgingly go, saying, "Well, you can make me go to bed, but you can't make me sleep!") and she would be up early every morning.

It was Jodie who brought Joan Baez to Camp Casey to help keep everyone's spirits up. It was Jodie who hooked me up with my dear friend and hero Martin Sheen, and she always seemed to have someone inspiring like Ed Asner or Ralph Nader lined up for me to speak to. She wasn't the one who put me in touch with Jesse Jackson, but the reverend would call me frequently to pray with me at bedtime, which meant so much to me. I was wound so tightly and the rev's prayers were extremely welcome.

Jodie stayed with me in the heat and ditches for almost the

entire month. She never complained, she never wanted any celebrity, she literally gave me the sandals off her feet, and she did it all for peace. She did it because she believed in what we were doing at Camp Casey, and we are still and always will be friends for life.

Johnny Wolf also became a close and dear friend of mine during the Camp Casey action in August. One of the founders of the Crawford Peace House, Johnny is one of the most calm and centered spirits I have ever met. He glides through life with a tranquillity that comes from his years of spiritual study and practice. Taking his cues and composure from many ancient spiritual teachers and traditions, he would often come to me, usually when I was in my most highly uncentered place, and say, "Poem break," in a voice that sounded remarkably like Tommy Chong's of Cheech and Chong. (As a matter of fact, Johnny and Hadi think the comedy duo should play them in the Camp Casey movie.)

During our "poem breaks" Johnny would usually read or recite something from memory by Rumi, a fifteenth-century Persian poet. He would look at me with the book of poems in his hand and say: "Awww, my sister, this one is dangerous," and read me a poem like this:

These spiritual window-shoppers,
who idly ask, "How much is that?" Oh, I'm just
*   looking.*
They handle a hundred items and put them down,

shadows with no capital.

What is spent is love and two eyes wet with weeping.

But these walk into a shop,

and their whole lives pass suddenly in that moment,

in that shop.

Where did you go? "Nowhere."

What did you have to eat? "Nothing much."

Even if you don't know what you want,

buy something, to be part of the exchanging flow.

Start a huge, foolish project,

like Noah.

It makes absolutely no difference

what people think of you.

"We Are Three," *Mathnawi* VI, 831–845

All of the poems Johnny read to me were classified by him as either "dangerous" or "fun." Our poem breaks were as welcome and appreciated as the rev's bedtime prayers!

When I finally returned to Crawford at Thanksgiving to re-unite with my new lifelong friends, after I hugged and kissed Johnny, he said, "My wife is jealous of you. One time when I was talking about you, she said, 'Why don't you divorce me, marry Cindy, and you two can move to Crawford and open a water park?' " Apparently Johnny talks about me too much to his wife!

When Johnny rescued me from the virulent attack of

Ma/Bro and MFSO, we jumped into his beat-up pickup truck and he looked at me and said, "Do you feel like crying?" I nodded my head and started crying and he said, "Mind if I join you?" and he started crying, too. I will love and treasure Johnny's friendship forever, whether we build that water park or not.

I contrast Johnny and Jodie to Ma/Bro. Ma/Bro often warned me that, after Camp Casey, my "new" friends would abandon me. Quite the contrary, it was Ma/Bro who abandoned me. The difference between them is that Johnny and Jodie can keep what is really important in focus: ending the occupation of Iraq. Ma/Bro could only keep me and what they think is my newfound fame and fortune in focus, and they wanted a piece of that "fame" without having to sweat in the ditches or take any of the smear on themselves.

The day after Ma/Bro got there was the worst day of the entire month. I had a fever and a horrible sore throat and my heart was broken by my dear friends coming and trying to fix a situation that wasn't broken, and taking what was working so well and trying to mold it into their idea of what a peace camp should look like. I told Ma/Bro how much they had hurt me and if they wanted to stay to support what we were trying to do, they were welcome, but if they wanted to undermine our efforts by their ego trips, they could turn around and go home. They stayed, and they didn't attack me to my face anymore, just behind my back at meetings and every other chance they could get.

We had many GSFP and MFSO members come to Camp Casey, and most of them were hugely supportive, especially Bill

Mitchell, who would never buy into the Cindy-bashing of Ma/Bro et al., but who would just pitch in and do whatever he could to stand beside me and to work to end the war.

The day I returned to Camp Casey after my mom's stroke, I was feeling really excited to be back. My attention had definitely been divided among my mom and my family and my thoughts of the people back in Crawford. When I left to rush home to California to be by my mom's side, I left a very crowded Camp I down by the triangle in the ditches, and when I came back I returned to Camp II, a couple of miles up the road and right near one of the checkpoints to Bush's faux ranch.

Camp II was a marvel. There was a chapel tent, a new volunteer station, a full kitchen with volunteer caterers, about a dozen Porta Potties, and a tent big enough to seat over five hundred people. I was walking through the tent admiring everything when I saw a huge portrait of Casey hanging in the back. I couldn't believe I hadn't noticed it before. I was so overcome with the vastness of what Casey had done that I almost collapsed.

By my boy's sacrifice, the peace movement in America crystallized and came into sharp focus and finally received the media attention that it deserved. My boy was the catalyst that galvanized the peace movement—it wasn't me, and no matter how much I kid, it wasn't George Bush.

Casey Sheehan is the anti–George Bush. Casey bravely served his country in the military; George did not. Casey worked his way through school and had nothing handed to him; George failed at everything he did and had everything handed to him. Casey was a faithful Christian filled with the spirit of the Christ; George is a hypocrite who says he is a Christian but then murders our brothers and sisters indiscriminately. Casey never abused alcohol or a single drug his entire life; well, we all know George did. How dare this person kill my son?

At the end of Camp Casey, more than fifteen thousand Americans and people from all over the world had come to stand with us in miserably hot Crawford, Texas. Hundreds upon hundreds of Texans came to show their disdain for a carpetbagger Texan who they think of as a silver-spoon Yankee who has exploited their state for his political gain. I teased everyone from Austin that I thought their entire city had come to join us! In fact, our first stop on the "Bring Them Home Now" tour when we left Camp Casey on August 31 was Austin. Thousands of Austinians came to cheer us and march with us. They roared in approval when I mentioned that I just might run for mayor!

The visitors that I treasured the most, though, were the soldiers who came from Fort Hood. One handsome young soldier came with his girlfriend almost every night when he got off work. He heard one day on Air America that we needed tarps, and he "borrowed" some from Fort Hood for us. I think the U.S. Army unknowingly provided us with other supplies, but I am not 100 percent sure about that. But thank you anyway, Uncle Sam! Our tax dollars at work.

Dozens of soldiers came to me to tell me to keep doing what I am doing to end the war, because they, too, felt ill-used and lied to about the so-called mission. They all told me that they knew that the war was for oil and bullshit. The soldiers told me that they didn't want to go, or in some cases, to go back.

One ex-soldier who was stationed at Fort Hood during Operation Iraqi Bullshit but who now was a civilian worker there, came out to Camp Casey on the second Sunday I was there. He brought three pictures of his buddies who had been killed in Iraq. We proudly hung the photos, next to which he had laminated with care, pictures of our other fallen heroes. We could all tell that he cared deeply about his "men" who hadn't come back to the States. At first glance, he looked like a hard-core ex-soldier who would be opposed to what we were doing, but he was actually very supportive and loving. The ex-soldier gave me a smooth stone that had the First Cavalry symbol—the black outline of a horse's profile on a yellow background—painted on it. He told me, and it meant so much to me, "Your son was a good soldier and so are you. He would be so proud of you." We hugged and cried: him for his losses, me for mine.

When I say I cried for my losses, you may think that I have only lost Casey. But so many things were killed when our child was killed: our family, our souls, our future, our happy past— not just our child.

When Jodie would send me off to bed after I had dutifully blogged, I would lie there all night, staring in an almost catatonic stupor of exhaustion and worry. Sometimes, unbeknownst to Jodie, I would sneak out and find some other insomniacs to drink beer and shoot the shit with. One of my midnight buddies was Jesse Dyen, who wrote and performs the song "Your Sons and Daughters," which became the Camp Casey theme song. I heard it for the first time the night I got back from Los Angeles. I had wrapped myself in a blanket and walked out to the big tent, where a group of people were sitting around one of the tables. Someone said, "Jesse, sing your song for Cindy." That's the first time I heard it. These are the words:

How 'bout your son
How 'bout your daughter
How come it's always poor folk
Who get shuffled off to slaughter
If you're so gung ho
Why don't you just go

In August of '05
A mighty voice did rise
She lost her precious son
And it can't be undone
She went to see the king
A downright simple thing
She thought she'd tell him of
The depth of a mother's love

How 'bout your son
How 'bout your daughter
How come it's always poor folk

Who get shuffled off to slaughter
If you're so gung ho
Why don't you just go
And send us back our sons and our daughters
Send us back our sons and our daughters

Here comes the smear campaign
She must love Saddam Hussein
Well, Mr. President
Why are you so hell-bent
On keeping up the lie
'Bout why our soldiers die
What is this noble cause
For which our young march off

How 'bout your son
How 'bout your daughter
How come it's always poor folk
Who get shuffled off to slaughter
If you're so gung ho
Why don't you just go
And send us back our sons and our daughters
Send us back our sons and our daughters

So why not answer her
What cause her son died for
If you're such a regular guy

PEACE MOM

Just look her in the eye
'Cause this ain't make believe
Beware the web you weave
Now go and fix your facts
'Cause we've got Cindy's back

How 'bout your son
How 'bout your daughter
How come it's always poor folk
Who get shuffled off to slaughter
If you're so gung ho
Why don't you just go
And send us back our sons and our daughters
Send us back our sons and our daughters
Send us back our sons and our daughters

One night I was actually falling asleep in my trailer after a wonderful woman had come in and given me a massage and soothed me with her amazingly sweet and calm voice. I was lying in bed, for once relaxed enough to sleep, when my cell phone rang: I know I should have turned it off, but I didn't want to miss a call from one of my children. By then, I had a new number that only family and close friends knew.

It was my friend Judy from Arizona. I couldn't fucking believe she was calling me at 2 A.M. After I answered, I think I said something like, "I can't fucking believe that you are calling me so late!" She had a habit of calling me when she was wild with some new worry, which was always baseless.

She practically screamed, "Why didn't you tell me Pat had filed for divorce?!"

"Because he didn't," I answered her.

"He did, he did. It's all over the Internet," she said, crying.

Well, there went my two hours of sleep for that night.

I immediately called Pat to find out what the hell was going on.

I haven't ever told him this, but until he filed for divorce and put our problems right in front of the right wing, those perfect people who have never said "fuck" or "shit," who have never gotten divorced or had any problems with their families, I was dying to come home and try to put our lives back together. I was tired of being separated and feeling so alone in the world. But then he filed for divorce. Every right-wing nut in the world had a good old time attacking me for that one. I know every Republican congressperson/senator/president surely never had any problems with his or her families or relationships. People like Rush or O'Reilly have never had drug problems or sexual harassment lawsuits filed against them. . . . That is why they feel so righteous in attacking other people for their life problems. It must be a heavy burden to be perfect.

Pat assured me that he had instructed his lawyer not to serve me with the divorce papers until we left Camp Casey. Somehow—no one knows how—news of the divorce was leaked to a right-wing blog. Hmm, I wonder how that happened. I believe Pat. He is an honorable man, even if he and I didn't see eye to eye on my work for peace.

So in the space of three short weeks, I became an internationally known media figure; I got served with divorce papers; several death threats were made against me; every right-wing hatemonger was spewing lies and filth about me; my mom had a stroke; and my husband's family sent out a press release supporting the president and denouncing me. If anyone was wondering why I didn't sleep much in August, you can stop wondering.

The press release was also something that my friend Judy had called to fill me in on. I knew my in-laws were rabid Republicans and that we never agreed on politics, but I figured at least we were all Catholic. When they voted for Bush in November and still believed the incredible bull-pucky that Casey died for was some kind of warped freedom, I couldn't talk to any of them. I knew that they wouldn't agree with my activism, but I falsely believed that they would support me. I had, after all, been in their family for twenty-eight years! I was beyond devastated when, on the sixth day of Camp Casey, my in-laws issued this press release:

> The Sheehan Family lost our beloved Casey in the Iraq War and we have been silently, respectfully grieving. We do not agree with the political motivations and publicity tactics of Cindy Sheehan. She now appears to be promoting her own personal agenda and notoriety at

the expense of her son's good name and reputation. The rest of the Sheehan Family supports our troops, our country, and our president, silently, with prayer and respect. Sincerely, Casey Sheehan's grandparents, aunts, uncles and numerous cousins.

Do you notice which relationships are *not* on this memo: Casey's brother, sisters, and father.

My sister-in-law recently e-mailed me and asked me to stop "talking" about this statement. That is easier said than done because I still get grilled about it all the time. "How does it feel that your own family doesn't support you?" Does this memo say that "my" family doesn't support me? No, it says that my husband's family doesn't support me. They are not my family anymore. And all I can say to that is: Thank God!

It would have been extremely nice and helpful to the entire family if the "Sheehan Family" had talked to me to find out what I was doing instead of writing about what it "appears" that I was doing. For them to take the side of a lying, greedy bastard instead of the mother of their own flesh and blood was supremely treacherous. I would never have done this to them. They had every right to do this according to the First Amendment, but according to the rules of family, they should never have done it. They upset my children, and they had no right to speak while invoking the name of their "beloved" Casey. When we moved to Northern California, they abandoned our family and had almost nothing to do with my children. Never even a birthday card. Okay, I didn't send my nieces and nephews cards either, but I wouldn't presume to exploit one of their deaths for my own political agenda, like the "Sheehan Family" did with Casey. He can't be their beloved Casey now, when he wasn't when he was alive.

A wife of one of Pat's cousins called a local right-wing radio show in Sacramento while I was at Camp Casey and told them that Casey joined the Army to get away from me because I was always a "liberal, feminist man-hater!" This is the same cousin who sent out a Christmas letter the year that Casey was killed lionizing her own family as if they were Greek gods and goddesses, but everything wasn't so great that year: their dog died! For God's sake, the same people who claimed a "beloved Casey" couldn't even mention that they had a cousin killed in Iraq! That was how beloved he was to them. Carly was so upset when she heard what Stepford Cousin said about me that she went on a local TV news program to tell America how close Casey and I were and how he used to call me at least once a day.

I would love to quit talking about the way my ex-family betrayed me, and I will when people stop attacking me about it.

Those nights when I couldn't sleep and I was able to move and leave my trailer were the most sacred nights at Camp Casey. There was no press around and most everyone was asleep, so I could move about Camp Casey without being mobbed and, with the regularity of Mickey Mouse at Disneyland, having pictures taken of me with our supporters. I loved meeting these people, I didn't mind the pictures or autographs, and Tiffany or

Alicia followed me to buffer the crowds and carry my gifts, but it got very exhausting. Especially since I was typically giving a dozen interviews every day. Toward the end, my trailer area had to be roped off so I could get into the tent without being surrounded. I had many nervous volunteer security and IVAW kids around me at all times, too.

But the nights that I ventured out into nocturnal Camp Casey were magical. The temperature was bearable by then and the night sky, unpolluted by smog or light, was carpeted with stars. And it was quiet, blessedly quiet. But there were always a few activists awake to drink beer with me and solve the world's problems. We wondered if the Secret Service could hear our conversations, which were always subversive, but nonviolently subversive. I would tease my fellow insomniacs that if they overslept reveille, Colonel Wright would have their asses in the morning!

Col. Ann Wright is another woman who was personally responsible for the success of Camp Casey. Ann single-handedly ran Camp Casey and organized the volunteers with the same competency and coolness that she had once used to evacuate embassies. She has become a lifelong friend and peace partner. I won't say much, but Ann's plots always involve horse manure. Ann is a remarkably stabilizing influence on me and the peace movement, even though she always wants to protest with horseshit!

The final week of Camp Casey found George out and about the country golfing, playing guitar, and eating birthday cake with John McCain while our country was experiencing its worst hurricane and people were hanging from their roofs in New Orleans and drowning in the toxic soup that was created when the levees broke. George was fully briefed on this, but days after the other needless destruction that his callous policies caused, he claimed that no one "anticipated" that the levees would burst—when this very same eventuality had been predicted with certainty for decades. Katrina was the final nail in his credibility coffin, but additional nails keep getting hammered in for good measure. Katrina was all I needed to dispute the fact that his Iraq policies were keeping our country "safer." Bollocks!

On the last day of Camp Casey, we were busy packing and I was giving final interviews, and we were all walking around with dark clouds over our heads. The day before, George had also confirmed my other suspicions by saying that we were in Iraq to "secure the oil fields from the terrorists." We all knew it was for oil: nice to have his confirmation. We were also sad because we had to leave what had turned out to be an amazing twenty-six days. Twenty-six days that would make history and be the catalyst for positive social change. We felt we had succeeded beyond anyone's wildest dreams.

I cried when I said good-bye to my media friends and the others who wouldn't be going on the Bring Them Home Now tour with us. The Bring Them Home Now tour was a natural extension of Camp Casey. We were struggling to think of how we could extend the feeling and the momentum of Camp Casey. We decided that some of us would go on tours throughout the country to take Camp Casey out to America—to the people who couldn't come to Crawford. I knew we would meet up again in D.C. on September 24 for the antiwar rally that was to draw over half a million people. I cried because I knew I was saying good-bye to the most insane but happiest summer of my life.

No matter how often we return to Crawford, nothing will ever compare to the "Summer of 2005." I wish the vigil hadn't been necessary, I wish it hadn't been necessary for me to be there—here's to hoping antiwar actions will soon become unnecessary. But peace activities will always be done.

From the first big rally on August 13, when we had our *Field of Dreams* experience as hundreds of cars lined Prairie Chapel Road for miles to drive from Crawford to Camp Casey, to the last rally on August 27, when busloads of attendees came on the second-hottest day of our vigil, we who stayed the entire month were constantly overwhelmed by the stories of commitment and sacrifice each and every attendee shared with us.

We left Camp Casey on the morning of August 31, outlasting George Bush by a few hours. He had decided to finally cut his vacation short and attend to his duties as president.

Four buses took off from Crawford. One went to New Orleans to establish Camp Casey, Covington, with five tons of leftover supplies, food, and water from Camp Casey, Crawford. The veterans on that bus got there and were often the first ones into communities with aid. Michael Moore shut down his New York office and sent his staff and raised more than $500,000 to use as hurricane relief. I will never give to the Red Cross again after having seen the grass-roots movements helping in New Orleans.

About six VFP members set up camp in Covington, Louisiana, and more and more volunteers arrived each day to help them help the people that Bush forgot about. About ten days after the hurricane, Alicia, Jeff, and I took a day off from the tour to go to Covington and see what the "boys" had been doing.

The work was incredible. The Camp Casey crew had hooked up with Malik Rahim, who would eventually found the Common Ground Collective that would provide significant relief to the people of New Orleans and the surrounding area, especially the poor. Although my visit to New Orleans was brief, I could smell the death and corruption that the hurricane and its aftermath had caused. I saw the machine-gun nests of our military and the heavily armored vehicles and command posts, and I was stunned to realize that this is what martial law looks like. It was also a frightening experience to realize that the destruction of New Orleans started many years ago, long before Katrina, and to realize how racist our country still is.

Our other three buses left to travel the country for the Bring Them Home Now tour.

We visited fifty cities and organized over two hundred events to continue Camp Casey and spread the love out all over the country.

I hopped from bus to bus, driving to a different city every day. It was hectic but fun traveling with my huge, gay marine friend Jeff Key, who acted as my bodyguard, and with Alicia, who was my capable assistant and friend for the tour.

All of the buses met in Washington, D.C., for the largest peace rally to date during this war. We set up Camp Casey, D.C., and welcomed over five hundred thousand other peace activists who joined with us in protest over the war.

The Camp Casey movement is still going and will never die. Even when our troops come home, we will keep it going to make sure this never happens again.

No more wars for greed that kill generations.

I won't let it happen to my grandchildren. Or yours.

Chapter 11

The Media

No government ought to be without censors,
and where the press is free, no one ever will.
— THOMAS JEFFERSON, LETTER TO GEORGE WASHINGTON,
SEPTEMBER 9, 1792

I WAS NEVER MUCH OF A NEWSHOUND UNTIL 9/11;
after 9/11 I couldn't get enough of the news. I usually watched
CNN . . . but could be persuaded on occasion to watch even Fox
News. I didn't realize then that we were being fed our daily
dosage of propaganda no matter what channel we were watching. After the invasion of Iraq, with everything that I had at
stake, I began to pay closer attention.

I never imagined in my wildest dreams that I would simultaneously become the darling and the demon of the media. That
I would be on a first-name basis with cameramen and sound
technicians. That I would experience media bias firsthand and
be in the middle of a media circus that rivaled any other up to
that time.

The media attention I received in Crawford was overwhelming and a lot of the time disheartening. I had been trying for months to break into the mainstream media to highlight the abuses of the Bush administration and to underscore the fact that the MSM routinely strives, I believe in agreement with our leaders, to keep Iraq out of the sight of Middle America.

Before the war started, I saw the MSM supporting the insane rush to war by not asking the president and his war council the tough questions. Why are you saying that Iraq has WMD when the U.N. weapons inspectors say it doesn't? Why are you linking Saddam with 9/11 when Osama bin Laden and al Qaeda have been identified by you as the perpetrators of that crime? Why are you heading pell-mell to disaster and sending our brave troops to fight, die, and kill in a country that doesn't appear to be an imminent threat to the national security of our country? These questions and others could have been asked . . . and asked . . . and asked until they were answered satisfactorily. Whatever happened to investigative reporting?

The MSM reported the "shock and awe" campaign in March of 2003, but the huge protests worldwide against this war in February of 2003 barely initiated a .01 on the Richter scale of importance to George Bush or to the MSM. The MSM also didn't report on the tragic loss of so many civilian lives in "shock and awe" and the subsequent invasion. The MSM has gone along with the Defense Department's policy of not counting "collateral damage." The MSM has also gone along with not reporting or focusing on torture, except to show some pictures of seemingly normal Americans committing abnormal and inhumane atrocities on fellow human beings. The Abu Ghraib torture scandal that a true investigative journalist and courageous reporter, Seymour Hersch, exposed in May of 2004, should have blown this scandalous war right apart, but the media went along and buried the story, along with its other victims.

I have also witnessed reporters and camerapersons being pushed around by law enforcement, and the media reps allow themselves to be pushed away and allow the government to take away their rights and our rights to a free press. The media buys into the fact that they can't take pictures of our dead heroes coming home from Iraq, and there is a ban on all photographs of these tragic occurrences. In New York City, when I was being arrested in March, the media obediently stayed behind an artificial line that the NYPD created for them. In almost every instance we Americans have been complicit in allowing our government to trample on our press. The press is not free in BushWorld.

There have been so many other events in the history of this invasion and occupation of Iraq that should have been hammered on by the media, but instead they get their feather dusters out and give Bush a light dusting and go on to the next celebrity scandal. I can think of so many: when Bush talked about the yellow-cake uranium at the 2003 State of the Union address; when Valerie Plame was "outed" in retaliation for her husband, Ambassador Joe Wilson, calling BushCo on that lie; when George declared "an end to major combat" in Iraq on May

1, 2003; when the 9/11 commission report came out, followed by the Senate Intelligence Report, and the Duelfer lack-of-WMD report; the Downing Street Memos. . . . Shall I continue, or are we getting the picture?

In September of 2004, the one-thousandth American soldier was killed in Iraq. The news that week was all about Scott Peterson being found guilty of murdering his wife and unborn baby. The media showed hundreds of people in front of the courthouse waving signs and screaming with bloodthirsty joy when he was found guilty. I wondered to myself then . . . when is the public going to come out in those great numbers to protest the war, and when will the thousand soldiers and their families that this callous excuse for an administration sent over to die in an immoral war gain justice for the crimes against us? When will the people of Iraq finally be able to live in peace?

In January of 2005, I was slated to appear on *Larry King Live* after the elections in Iraq. I was going to be asked if I thought Casey's sacrifice was "worth it." I thought that was a fair question and I was prepared to go in with both guns blazing and ask Larry if he would have one of his children killed on the altar of greed for sham elections. All of my preparation went for naught, though, when I was bumped because the Michael Jackson child molestation trial started that day.

I went to Crawford, Texas, on August 6, 2005, not to start a media shit storm but to ask George Bush one simple question: "What noble cause did my son die for?" I didn't plan, or even realize, that the MSM would be out there in force and very bored. I should have seen where this was going, though, when I was on Wolf Blitzer the first morning after I sat in the ditch. His producer in Crawford told me, "You planned this perfectly, there's nothing going on."

I said, "Oh, really, there's nothing going on? Twenty-four soldiers and Marines were killed in Iraq this week. Tell their families there's nothing going on."

She replied, "Well, you know what I mean."

No, I didn't know what she meant. Iraq should always be on the front pages of every paper and the lead story of every news program whether there is a mom sitting in a ditch in Crawford or not. The media has gone along with the government in sanitizing this war for everyone. Like Barbara Bush said, she doesn't want to bother her "beautiful mind" with such things as returning caskets.

Another irony of Crawford was that the media joyfully and, I believe, spitefully scrutinized everything I have ever written, said, or done. I am just a mom from California trying to end a war before any other moms have their hearts and souls ripped out. George Bush never gets scrutinized for saying that Saddam had WMD and that they could be on the East Coast in forty-five minutes. I also found it highly ironic that most of the media representatives who came to Crawford privately supported me but publicly castigated or ridiculed me.

I have been hoping against hope that it wouldn't "get out,"

but now I know I must confess it: In second grade, I called my teacher, Miss McMurray, a "fat poop-head." Everything comes back to haunt me!

I believe the media is partly responsible for the invasion and our continued presence in Iraq. They still won't ask the hard questions, but particularly: "What noble cause?" I also believe that everyone in America has bloody hands from this monstrosity, some bloodier than others. If the MSM did its job we never would have invaded Iraq, and if it would do its job now we would be getting out of there sooner.

One day at Camp Casey, I was on Anderson Cooper's show from a remote hookup. I accused the media of not asking the tough questions of the president and reminded him of the media's complicity in the continued slaughter of innocents in Iraq. He said, "Well, we can only ask the questions so many times." I wondered aloud what happened to "investigative reporting." I didn't realize it then, but it was "on" between me and baby-blue-eyed Anderson Cooper.

He took on investigating me with a vengeance. He dredged up everything I ever did or said. He came down to Camp Casey with his crew one day to do a hatchet job on me.

First, he had Dana Bash, another CNN reporter, on to talk about the Camp Casey phenomena—she is a nice lady, and I don't remember what she said. Then he had me on. The first question was, "Is it true you called George Bush a terrorist?" Well, of course it is true. I have never denied that he is a terrorist. I don't remember much of the interview after that, but I do know the rest of his show was filled with "Cindy haters." I left to go to the Peace House right after the Cooper debacle, but I hear that my sister had to be restrained from beating Anderson up, and the person who was helping me with publicity called one of his other guests a "stupid asshole."

I also had many horrifying experiences with Fox and Rush Limbaugh while I was at Camp Casey.

One of the first days I was there, Bill O'Reilly called me a "traitor" on his show and then the next day was begging me to be on it. I told one of my assistants that I would be happy to be on his show if he would publicly apologize for calling me a traitor. I have yet to be on his show, but he still criticizes me and lies about me every chance he gets. I really think it is getting to the point now that, just like a little third-grade boy, he wants to kiss me and doesn't know how to say it.

After I was arrested at the State of the Union address for exercising my First Amendment right to free speech, Bill O'Reilly called me "a known militant" and said he was *sure* I was going to do something. If I *was* going to do something, wouldn't I have taken off my jacket during the president's speech? What he was saying was that it is okay to arrest somebody for thinking something. Or does he think it's okay to be bombing a country back to the Stone Age because we somehow *know* that Saddam wanted WMD? The right-wing smear machine is despicable and I hardly ever give them a second thought. However, some of the things that they say about me are so egregious, I just have to laugh, or rebut them.

One of the weirdest things that came out of a hatemonger's mouth was when Rush Limbaugh said that I was just like Bill Burkett, who supposedly gave forged documents to CBS in regard to Bush's already well-known cowardice during Vietnam. Rush said that my own story "is based on false documents." How dare he say anything like that, and how dare anyone still listen to the blowhard drug addict? What in fuck's sake does he think I did? Bury an empty coffin on April 13, 2004, so I could deviously go to the president's fake ranch one year and four months later and hold him responsible for my imaginary son's death? Rush Limbaugh should rot in whatever hellish afterlife he has made for himself, or at least be abjectly ashamed for that careless and callous remark.

Rush Limbaugh also gave me some grudging respect for continuing to speak out against Hillary Clinton because he is sure that the Clintons kill people who disagree with them. He said I either had a lot of courage or stupidity.

The media holds shiny keys in one hand to distract our country from the crimes in Iraq, but some publications and media outlets shine the spotlight directly on the crimes. I came to love even more Air America, the blogs, *The Lone Star Iconoclast, Democracy Now!* and Amy Goodman, Truthout.org, Michael Moore, LewRockwell.com, commondreams.org, and much of the international media, who not only gave me a fair shake, but were very supportive of me.

The Lone Star Iconoclast's reporting from Camp Casey was always balanced and fair. The one day when the "anti-Sheehan" crowd came, the *Iconoclast* interviewed many people from the other side and gave the country great insight into the motivations of these individuals.

The reader may remember the *Iconoclast* as the Crawford area newspaper that endorsed John Kerry for president in 2004 with a scathing editorial excoriating its readers' neighbor, the Rhinestone Cowboy, George Bush. Leon Smith, the editor said, among other things:

> We should expect that a sitting President would vacation less, if at all, and instead tend to the business of running the country, especially if he is, as he likes to boast, a "wartime president." America is in service 365 days a year. We don't need a part-time President who does not show up for duty as Commander-In-Chief until he is forced to, and who is in a constant state of blameless denial when things don't get done.

In the end, we just want fairness in reporting. The MSM's slant is always pro-war, and the pro-peace view rarely gets an audience with Middle America. I am glad that the reporters and other media persons were bored that August and got the message out to America. In a rare instance, but for the wrong reasons, the MSM did a good thing. Thousands of Americans came out in support of Camp Casey and millions who couldn't come kept up with our activities through the MSM and especially the *Iconoclast,* which blogged almost constantly from our peace camp.

If we are to have a free and informed society, we must have a free press. A free press, envisioned by our nation's founders, should be another way to check our government. When most of the media are complicit with the government, the government gets out of control and then we the people have to rein in the government and the media.

I was not afraid to take on the press for the same reason that I am not afraid to take on King George and his kangaroo court: I buried my oldest child.

I was reading an analysis of my media impact one day and the analyst said that if only I had gone home and been quiet after Camp Casey, that I would have gone down in media history as being a very effective person. But by staying active in the media, I had become a "caricature" of myself.

Obviously, this analyst didn't comprehend the fact that I did not go to Crawford to garner any kind of media attention: I went to Crawford on August 6 to ask the president a question that he still hasn't answered. I started my mission on April 4 to bring to the attention of the country the facts that we were at war and some horrible things were being done in our name.

I went to Crawford as an extension of what I had been doing over the previous year: calling for an end to the occupation of Iraq.

Iraq is still being occupied.

Cindy Sheehan

My mission isn't about breaking into the media, or having my "fifteen minutes of fame."

It is about truth.

It is about democracy.

It is about our essential human rights.

It is about creating a paradigm of peace in our country and in our world.

When all of these issues are resolved, then I will go away.

Not a minute before.

Chapter 12

A New World
Is Possible

Yes, we did produce a near perfect Republic.
But will they keep it, or will they, in the enjoyment
of plenty, lose the memory of freedom?
Material abundance without character is
the surest way to destruction.

—THOMAS JEFFERSON

WE NEED A NEW WORLD. THIS ONE IS BROKEN.

Before Casey was killed in Iraq on April 4, 2004, I never traveled much to speak of. I had gone to Israel and Mexico and that was about it. I had a barely used passport.

Since I began to speak out against the dishonesty and deception that led to this illegal and morally reprehensible occupation of Iraq, I have journeyed all over the United States and am now starting to fill my passport with stamps.

Our world is so beautiful and the humans who inhabit it are

203

for the most part loving. All they want is a good life for themselves and their children. They just want to feel safe and secure in their communities. They want to be warm and fed. They want clean drinking water and they want to dance and laugh when appropriate. They want to live long lives with their families and they want their children to bury *them* at the end of their time here. In short, the people of the world want what we Americans want.

It is our governments who want to demonize and marginalize other cultures, religions, races, and ethnic groups. George Bush and his coldhearted cronies and his easily misled and willingly blind followers want to "fight them over there so we don't have to fight them over here!" Who are these "thems" that we are fighting over there? Are they the babies lying in their cribs when a bomb (chemical or conventional) is dropped on their house? Is it the mother who has gone shopping for her family's daily food and is killed by a car bomber who never even thought to commit such a heinous act until his country was occupied by a foreign invader? Is it the grandmas and grandpas who are too old, or too stubborn, to leave their lifelong homes when the coalition troops are carpet-bombing innocent cities?

We as citizens of the United States of America must stop allowing our leaders to give the orders to kill innocent people. I almost said, We must stop allowing our leaders to "kill" innocent people. But we all know the cowards don't fight their own fantasy battles or send their own children to fight in the causes that they idiotically and diabolically call "noble." No, they order our children to go over and do their dishonest and destructive dirty work. Our soldiers are taught that "Hajis," the brown-skinned people of Iraq who clean their toilets, showers, and wash their clothes, are less than people . . . which enables them to be killed more easily. The dehumanization of the Iraqi people is also dehumanizing our soldiers. Our children.

I once got a letter from a "patriotic American" who told me that when we see the mothers and fathers of Iraq screaming because their babies have been killed, that they "are just acting for the cameras. They are animals who don't care about their children because they know they can produce another." This is another example of the mentality of General Sheridan when he said, "the only good Indian is a dead Indian." This sort of wicked rhetoric dehumanizes us all.

A new world is necessary, but it can be possible only if we believe and live the belief that every human being is inherently the same as we are. They feel pain when they are hurt. They have hunger pangs when they haven't eaten. Their mouths go dry when they are thirsty. They mourn when they experience a loss. They shiver when they are cold. They laugh when they are happy. How can we condone, or even allow, our leaders to kill our brothers and sisters like this?

A new world is necessary, and it can be possible only if we rein in the depraved corporations that thrive off of the flesh and blood of our neighbors all over the world and here in America. War profiteers like Halliburton, Bechtel, and General Electric are racking up obscene profits and increasing the bottom line for their shareholders while they are running roughshod over this planet. Malevolent companies such as Dow are dumping chemicals and other pollutants into the water and atmosphere that kill people, our environment, and our future! Companies like Wal-Mart are exploiting workers in the United States and abroad to enrich a family that already has more than enough money to fund health care and a living wage for all of its employees—and have a little extra left over to pay their own country club fees.

A new world is necessary, and it can be possible only if we decrease our dependency on oil and use some of the money that we are pouring into the desert sands and sewers of Iraq to expand research on renewable energy sources and expound and promote the renewable sources we already have, such as biodiesel fuels. I have talked to many citizens of Venezuela who are understandably nervous about a U.S. invasion and they know that such an action would not be because President Chavez is a "dictator"—he is not—he is a democratically elected leader who is very popular in his own country. The people of Venezuela are savvy, and they know that if the United States invades their country it won't be because we are spreading "freedom and democracy" to them. They know they already have it.

A new world is necessary but not possible until we Americans get over the arrogant idea that we alone can solve the massive problems of Iraq and of human-rights violations. We have to reach out to fellow members of the human race all over the world to forge the bonds that are crucial to protecting innocent people who are impoverished or targeted by our government and corporatism that has gone wild and is largely unchecked.

Peace and justice are intimately connected, and the world can't have one without the other.

A new world is possible and it is attainable. For this new world to be made real, we need to take into our beings what Martin Luther King, Jr., once said when he was imagining his own eulogy:

> I'd like somebody to mention that day, that Martin Luther King, Jr., tried to give his life serving others. I'd like for somebody to say that day, that Martin Luther King, Jr., tried to love somebody. I want you to say that day, that I tried to be right on the war question. I want you to be able to say that day that I did try in my life to clothe those who were naked. I want you to say on that day that I did try in my life to visit those who were in prison. I want you to say that I tried to love and serve humanity. Yes, if you want to say that I was a drum major, say that I was a drum major for justice. Say that I was a drum major for peace. I was a drum major for righteousness.

I would like someone to say these same things about me one day.

Chapter 13

Peace Mom

Matriotism and Pacifism

Everyone's a pacifist between wars.
It's like being a vegetarian between meals.
—COLMAN McCARTHY

I HAD ALWAYS BEEN A BASICALLY (*BASICALLY* WAS ONE
of Casey's favorite words) peaceful person. I was like Casey; I
never even got into one fistfight with a person who wasn't my
brother or sister. I avoided conflicts at all costs. I don't think
I could have been considered a "chicken," but I just never believed that anything positive could be accomplished by violence.

I think I may have been opposed to conflict because I grew
up in a home where conflict was the norm. If my mom and dad
weren't yelling at each other, they weren't speaking to each
other. My brother and sister and I were often verbally and/or
physically abused by our parents. Name calling was normal in
our home, too.

When I grew up and raised my own children, I vowed that we would never use violence to solve problems. We treated each other with respect no matter what age we were. Even the parents said *please* and *thank you* to the children, and the children were respectful to the parents and each other. Often we would talk about problems the children were having with other children, adults, or teachers, and I would emphasize to our children over and over that even if another person was rude to them, they had to be polite to the rude person in return. The "f"-word was definitely a no-no in our home. But all of this changed when Casey was killed.

I was a history major in college and I grew up during the Vietnam War. I knew the violent history of our country, but I believed that there were three "good" wars: the Revolutionary War, the Civil War, and World War II. I have since studied these conflicts from a perspective shaped by having a child killed in war, and I realized that all war is wrong; and no, just because I now believe that the Civil War was wrong, I am not a racist. And just because I believe now that World War II was wrong does not make me anti-Semitic.

When people accuse me of being a Roosevelt "basher" and being anti-Semitic, I must remind them that Georgie's grampy, Prescott, funded and supported the Nazis, and America turned back scores of refugee Jews from Europe. The prison camps weren't liberated until the end of the war, after many millions of Jews, Christians, and dissenters had been tortured and exterminated. After Roosevelt died, his successor, Harry Truman, actually committed mass murder and war crimes in Japan using two nuclear weapons that killed tens of thousands of people in two days, and many more died slow deaths from radiation poisoning and disease. HST should have been tried for crimes against humanity, but the monster that came out on top lived to get our country into another immoral war, an undeclared war: Korea.

Since World War II, the United States has been involved in one illegal and undeclared conflict after another, the biggest ones being Korea, Vietnam, Kosovo, Panama, and the two wars against Iraq—not to mention our covert wars in South America and Asia, and our support of the mujahideen (for which Osama was a major combatant) in Russia's war against Afghanistan.

So, another strange transformation that I have made in the last two years is one from a "peaceful" person who vaguely disliked violence to a fierce pacifist who believes that all war is wrong and unnecessary and preventable. I believe that in this, the twenty-first century, killing to solve problems, especially imaginary problems, is barbaric and insane.

I believe that any country has the right to defend its citizens when attacked, but the Iraq "war," and every other ill-advised war that our country has ever fought, has never been about keeping America safer. As a matter of fact, every war has led to the next one and to the pointless death of our young people and innocent citizens of other countries.

If we don't finally wake the hell up as a human race and loudly repudiate any attacks on fellow humans who just happen to be our "enemies" because they live within different bound-

aries than the ones we live in, our existence is doomed. Martin
Luther King Jr. said, "It is either peaceful coexistence, or violent
annihilation." We are slowly killing ourselves by war, and we
allow our leaders—mostly male white ones—to march our children off to war to kill each other.

Much as I wish I could take credit for the word *matriotism,*
another woman wrote to me and gave me the concept. I was so
intrigued by the word that I have been meditating on the possible ideology behind it, and a new paradigm for true and lasting
peace in the world.

Before I delve into the concept of matriotism, let's explore
the word *patriotism.* Dictionary.com defines it as *love of country
and willingness to sacrifice for it.* But I think we all know that
patriotism in the United States means *exploiting others' love for
country by sending them to sacrifice for my bank balance!*

There have been volumes written about patriotism, defin-
ing it, supporting it, challenging the notion of it, etc. I believe
the notion of patriotism has been expediently and nefariously
exploited and used to lead our nation into scores of disastrous
and needless wars. The idea of patriotism has virtually decimated and weakened entire generations of our precious young
people and has enabled our nation's leaders to commit mass
murder. The vile sputum of "You're either with us or against us"
is basically the epitome of patriotism gone wild.

This sort of patriotism begins when we enter kindergarten
and learn the Pledge of Allegiance. It transcends all sense when
we are taught "The Star-Spangled Banner," a hymn to war. In

our history classes the genocide of the Native American peoples is glossed over as we learn about the spread of American imperialism over our continent, though it wasn't named until the 1840s, when the doctrine of Manifest Destiny was put forth to justify the USA's conquest and "civilizing" of Mexican territories and Native American populations. Manifest Destiny sought to spread the "boundaries of freedom" to the American continent, with the notion that we have a special mission from God. Sound familiar?

All through school, we are brainwashed into believing that somehow our leaders are always right and have our best interests at heart when they wave the flag and convince us to hate fellow human beings who stand in the way of their making immense profits from war. As Samuel Johnson said, "patriotism is the last refuge of a scoundrel."

Matriotism is the opposite of patriotism . . . not to destroy it, but to be a yin to its yang and to balance out the destructive militarism of patriotism.

Not everyone is a mother, but there is one universal truth that no one can deny or dispute no matter how hard he tries (and believe me, some will try): Everyone has a mother! Mothers give life, and if the child is lucky, mothers nurture life. And if a man has had a nurturing mother, he will also already have a sound basis for matriotism.

A matriot loves his or her country but does not buy such exploitive slogans as "My country, right or wrong." (As G. K. Chesterton said, that's like saying, "My mother, drunk or sober.") A matriot knows that her country can do a lot of things right, especially when the government is not involved. For example, I know of no other citizens of any country who are more personally generous than those of America. However, a matriot also knows that when her country is wrong, it can be responsible for murdering millions of people. A true matriot would never drop an atomic bomb, carpet bomb cities and villages, or control drones from thousands of miles away to kill innocent men, women, and children.

There is another thing that matriots would never do, however, and this is the key to stopping killing to solve problems: a matriot would never send her child or another mother's child to fight nonsense wars . . . and would herself march into a war that she considered just, in order to protect her child from harm. Aha! Matriots would fight their own battles, but take a dim view of having to do so, and they would seldom resort to violence to solve conflict. Patriots hide behind the flag and eagerly send young people to die in order to fill their own pocketbooks.

Women flocked to Camp Casey in August to run the huge enterprise and work for peace, and women from all over the United States and the rest of the world have invited me to visit and speak and advocate for true and lasting peace. Men who are in touch with the matriot inside them have also been vitally important to the cause of eradicating war.

There was Ann Wright, Jodie Evans, Barb Cummings, Alicia Sexton, Tiffany Burns, Sergeant Major Tammara, Lisa

Fithian, Dede Miller, and Rena (the office goddess) who gave up their entire summer to join me in our quest for truth. Camp Casey ran like a well-oiled machine because women ran it and the men willingly carried out our directives. It was an ideal society.

I know one thing from the bottom of my heart. My son, Casey, who was an Eagle Scout and a true American patriot, was not served well by his idea of patriotism. I will never forgive myself for not trying to counteract the false patriotism he was raised on with a true sense of matriotism.

I also know that the women of the world who don't have a voice, such as the mothers of Iraq who are struggling just to survive in their needlessly destroyed country, are counting on us women who do have voices to use them to end George Bush's *manifestly* idiotic *doctrine* of preemptive wars of aggression based on the justification that "I think that country might be dangerous to me and my pals. We better attack it and see how much money we can line our pockets with."

War will end forever when we matriots stand up and say, "No, I am not giving my child to the fake patriotism of the war machine, which chews up my flesh and blood to spit out profits."

As matriot Emma Goldman said, "Patriotism . . . is a superstition artificially created and maintained through a network of lies and falsehoods; a superstition that robs man of his self-respect and dignity, and increases his arrogance and conceit."

Matriotism above all is a commitment to truth and a celebration of the dignity of all life. Not just the unborn life that so many males seem to define as important. All life!

It is tough to be a pacifist during war because pacifists are so often accused of being traitorous——which really means antistate and antimurder. Pacifists need to stand up courageously during times of war and call all people back to their higher selves. If we can be pacifists during war, then perhaps we can prevent the next war and the killing of more of our children.

Chapter 14

From Camp Casey till Now

*"Your writing is like
a third-century Greek playwright."*
—DARIO FO, LONDON, DECEMBER 2005

MY WORLD HAS BEEN A CYCLONE OF PEACE ACTION and unbelievable events since I somewhat grudgingly left Crawford more than eight months ago and stepped into a life that is bizarrely exciting and yet simultaneously as exhausting and lonely as ever.

Since I am "single" again, I have had a few futile dates: the men acted more like fans than friends. It is so annoying to never know if you are being courted because of who you are or *who* you are.

I was sitting around a table one night at Camp Casey Thanksgiving with about five of my fellow peace activists—all men. I was lamenting that I didn't have a relationship right then. Yes, even though I am suddenly famous and travel all around the world, even though I have helped to create a phenomenal peace movement, even though I meet with world leaders and other dignitaries, I still worry about relationships and my kids. I still lie alone in bed every night, lonely after sharing a bed with Pat for twenty-eight years.

One of my pals said, "You must get at least one marriage proposal a day." Well, no. I have received only one proposal, from a very sweet letter carrier who came up to me after I spoke at the University of California at Berkeley. I don't even get asked out for coffee! Since I never spend more than one or two days in the same place, it's hard to strike up even a long-distance relationship. My pals were stunned: If they weren't all married, they would date me in a second, they swore! Sweet, but not exactly helpful!

Besides worrying about relationships, or the lack thereof, my life is one of constant, lonely travel. Sometimes I am on airplanes as often as three or four times a week. I have been told by pilots and flight attendants that I fly more then they do. There have been a few periods since Camp Casey when I have flown every day for two or three weeks in a row. One day I flew to Italy for a less than twenty-four-hour turnaround! I came back, stopped in Miami overnight, then headed to Venezuela.

In Venezuela, I was treated like a head of state. In Latin America I am called "Madre Coraje" (Mother Courage). President Hugo Chavez gave me a new name when I was down there: Mrs. Hope. That's in contrast to what he calls George Bush: Mr. Danger.

Dede and I were invited to Venezuela along with a few other peace activists, including Jodie and Medea, the cofounders of CodePink Women for Peace. I didn't know it until I got there, but the foreign ministry in Venezuela paid for my flight and my hotel and food. I did not go to Venezuela to meet with Chavez. I was invited to be a speaker at the World Social Forum and in fact spoke before a huge rally after a march that had people stretched for three miles. I couldn't see the end of the rally from the stage!

There is a funny anecdote from one of my speeches in Venezuela: I was giving my speech and it was being translated into Spanish by my translator, who stayed with me the entire time. He was a young Cuban named Enrique. At the end of my speech, I was saying, "You can be assured that there are people in America who are working really, really hard to hold George Bush accountable and have him impeached for all of his lies!" Enrique translated that into Spanish, and the crowd roared. I continued, "Then after he is impeached, he has to be removed from office!" Again it was translated, and the crowd went wild! Then to conclude, I said, "And after he is removed from office, he has to be tried for war crimes!" The crowd went insane and started chanting "Viva, Cindy!" I thought, "Wow, these people really love trials!"

I didn't know until I had left Venezuela and was in Customs

that I had been slightly mistranslated on my last sentence. When I said that Bush needed to be tried for war crimes, my translator had said: "He needs to be executed!" A bilingual American who was on the same flight with me ran up to relate that story to me. I am totally amazed that I haven't been smeared yet for calling for Bush's execution! So whenever I have to be translated now, I start by saying that I am a pacifist and I am against the death penalty, no exceptions!

When I was in Venezuela, President Chavez spent about an hour and a half with us and he agreed to help the peace movement, energizing nearly two million women from South America to sign on to our international call for the end to the occupation of Iraq.

I am often accused of having met with an "anti-American dictator." Hugo Chavez is not a dictator; he has been democratically elected to his office eight times, once after a coup attempt more than likely stirred up by the CIA. He is also not anti-American, he is anti–Mr. Danger. Besides, Hugo Chavez is an American. We Americans who live in the United States are so arrogant, we can't see past the ends of our noses to realize that everyone who lives in North America *or* South America is an American.

I was on Faux (Fox) News one Saturday afternoon from Los Angeles after my return from Venezuela. The anchor was admonishing me for meeting with Chavez and she said, "Human rights organizations say that his regime tortures people."

I was flabbergasted! "Our country imprisons people illegally and tortures people," I retorted. "I am calling on all leaders of all countries to repudiate human rights violations." At which point the interview was over—quickly! Besides, where do these anchors get off expressing their opinions? Just ask the damn questions!

I was on the WGN-TV news in Chicago, and near the end of the program they showed a picture of Hugo Chavez and me hugging, and the anchor said, "Some people say that this is your Jane Fonda moment."

"Oh, really," I responded, "I didn't know that we were at war with Venezuela." The anchor looked dumbfounded, as if I had taken away his lollipop. I could hear the director screaming in his ear to say something. I don't ever mind being compared to Jane Fonda, anyway. I think she is a great American who did a lot to call attention to the illegal and immoral war of her generation and end it sooner. All of the propaganda about prisoners being further tortured or killed because of her visit is false. Sometimes we push the envelope for peace, but I know that Jane (who is now a friend of mine) and I are willing to take the shit to save lives. The people who give us crap are the monstrous ones—people who perpetuate killing for their evil sport and profit.

If BushCo are going to spew the rubbish that we are spreading "freedom and democracy," we cannot allow them to pick and choose which democracies to support. Venezuela is a democracy, and the people who live there love Hugo Chavez, unless they were members of the "oil-garchy" who lost a lot of power and money when Chavez took over the running of the oil companies. He is helping the lower class raise its standard of living and he has been overwhelmingly elected in elections certified by international groups. That's all I need to know.

President Chavez is not the only foreign dignitary I have met with. I have met with parliamentarians all over the world and many congresspeople in our own country. When I met with Dermot Ahern, the foreign minister of Ireland (Condi's equivalent), or the vice president of Spain, I was also accused of sedition in a time of war. Of course, I haven't been accused of that by any actual law enforcement officials, just the court of the right-wing smear machine. Even supporters of mine said that it is okay to speak against the war and against BushCo at home, but when I go outside of the country to do so is wrong. This kind of reasoning is, of course, faulty.

Even Spain, who withdrew its troops from Iraq, is still supporting BushCo in their war crimes, as are Great Britain, Ireland, and Italy—all countries I have visited and where I have encouraged leaders not to support the crimes against humanity being committed by our country. I, as a good friend, would try to talk another friend out of hurting him- or herself or someone else if I knew what that friend was planning on doing. I believe that leaders of countries should do the same and not support another country in committing murder.

While I was speaking to Dermot Ahern, who is a true gentleman, he admitted that he was going to get in some trouble from D.C. for meeting with me, but he said he didn't care because "it is the right thing to do." He was trying to show me documents and prove that the war in Iraq was legal according to the Irish constitution and the U.N. Although he is intimately connected with the U.N. and is being whispered about to be the next secretary-general, I disputed his conclusion that the war was in any way legal.

Dermot Ahern is a staunch Catholic, and Ireland is a Catholic country where abortion is illegal and only the wealthy can cross the border to England to obtain legal abortions. I looked him straight in the eye and I said to him, "Mr. Secretary, abortion is legal in my country; does that make it moral?" I could tell that he was visibly moved and that my question went deeply into his soul.

Right after my trip to Ireland, I was invited to speak at an international peace conference in London. Ken Livingstone, the mayor of London and a vocal thorn in Blair's and Bush's side, hosted a reception in my honor at London's City Hall. That was where I discovered that Italian Playwright Dario Fo, who is a Nobel laureate, had written a play about my story called *Peace Mom.*

I was perusing a table with the requisite inventory of peace pins, bumper stickers, and flyers when I saw a bright yellow half-page flyer with a picture of a strange woman on it and the title *Peace Mom.* I thought, "Hey, what the heck? I'm the peace mom!" But as I read the flyer, I discovered that Dario Fo had written the play about me and it was starring Frances de la Tour as *me!*

I can't convey how surreal it was to sit in an audience with a legendary British stage actress playing me right next to a legendary playwright who wrote a play about me. And not just a play, but a play and performance that stunned everybody into an admiring silence. Dario Fo used my words and embellished a little to really capture the spirit of my righteous rage and the love and compassion of Camp Casey. In the Q and A afterward, Dario said that I had the same simplicity and honesty in my writing as one of the third-century Greek playwrights! I floated home from the play on air, and not because of the pint I drank in a nearby pub beforehand.

One day when we were in the middle of the Bring Them Home Now tour right after Camp Casey, I got a call from Jane Fonda. When we were in New York, she said she wanted to meet me personally and to meet my daughters. I had already met her daughter, Vanessa, when she and Eve Ensler came to Camp Casey in August. Eve wrote an amazing piece about me for *Oprah* magazine. Eve had to fight to get them to do an interview about me and they only agreed if there was to be no "Bush bashing" in the article.

So Carly, Janey, Dede, Jane, Vanessa, and I met for lunch, and my girls got a rare treat to be able to talk to Vanessa about what it was like to be the daughter of a famous "traitor." That has been Vanessa's fate for her entire life, but my girls were forced into the cause almost overnight. Vanessa tried to tell them to support me in every way they could, and not to listen to the negative, false stories. My sister got a picture of Jane and me together, and she is always threatening to sell it to *The National Enquirer* with the caption "Hanoi Jane and Baghdad Cindy plotting revolution." After that afternoon in New York, my girls decided that being the daughters of the Peace Mom could have some benefits! My daughter Janey was very ill from a cold, and she spent most of the time huddled in Jane Fonda's bed; Jane was serving her soup and bringing her orange juice and water. I heard Janey talking to one of her friends that day marveling about the whole thing.

One day I was sitting on Jodie's back porch in Venice, California (where I stay every time I am in Los Angeles—I even have my own room), with Dan Ellsberg and Jane's ex-husband, Tom Hayden: two courageous peace activists I studied about in school and who have made a huge difference in our world and in my life. I had known Tom since meeting him in D.C. during the Downing Street Memo hearings. We were having a conversation about politics and war and I was an active participant in the discussion—Dan and Tom actually cared about what I thought and said. I had one of my "where am I and who am I?" moments. I got slightly dizzy then thought to myself, "Wow, I am so sure, I am sitting here chatting and drinking beer with Daniel Ellsberg and Tom Hayden! If my history profs at UCLA could only see me now!"

My Jane Fonda moment was later followed by my Susan Sarandon moment. I found out shortly after Camp Casey that a few producers were looking into making a movie about the experience. We chose Jill Canaparo as the producer and started working on the movie. Jill is a great woman who not only produces movies and documentaries but is a practicioner of Chinese medicine and a very spiritual person. She called me one day with the astonishing news that Susan Sarandon was interested in playing me in the movie!

I finally got to meet Susan at a Bring Them Home Now concert in New York. I was one of the only speakers alongside such acts as Michael Stipe of REM, who became my favorite singer-songwriter that night. Susan and I met briefly and she introduced me. We got to know each other better at breakfast the next day.

Meeting Susan and the other celebrities at the concert was an amazing experience, but what amazed me the most about it was that the people who came to listen to the fabulous music were so receptive to me. There was a reception before the concert where people actually paid extra to meet me! Jeez—all I did was sit in a ditch. Everyone knows how to sit down. Look what happens when one stands up, or more appropriately, sits down for what one believes in. At the end of my speech I led a chant with my favorite march cadence, since I couldn't sing, dance, or even juggle. The chant goes: *"Violence and occupation do not bring liberation. That's bullshit, get off it. This war is for profit."*

It was a fun night, and I think I looked really cute in my brown puffy skirt, a pink T-shirt (an exact replica of the one I was arrested for wearing at the State of the Union Address in Congress), and a snazzy brown sweater with pink tights and sparkly brown shoes. Someone yelled out from the crowd, "You're a rock star!" I felt like a peace star that night!

There are a few perks to being a peace star to go along with the heartache and loneliness. For instance, I always get free goodies on planes: snacks, drinks, bottles of wine, headphones, and even sometimes upgrades.

I have an apartment that I don't have to pay for. It's really a place where my stuff can live since I am never there. But it is a cute little no-bedroom apartment in Berkeley up in the hills with a marvelous view of the bay. I live below two very generous peace activists, and I don't even have to pound on the ceiling with a broom too often when they are jumping up and down in their living room! Steve and Virginia (my upstairs friends, they won't let me call them landlords) often accompany me to peace events around the Bay Area and carry the gifts that I'm lucky enough to receive. We have another connection, though: Virginia, who is a very young, successful attorney, shares the same birthday with Casey.

Speaking of sharing the same birthday with Casey, I was at a feminist awards dinner once that honored four female Nobel Peace Prize winners. My friend Mimi Kennedy introduced me to Bob Hope's daughter, Linda. Mimi said: "I want you to meet Bob Hope's daughter, she is pretty conservative, but still, come and meet her." So I went over to Mimi's table and I introduced myself to Linda, and I told her that Casey was born on the same day as her father.

I know that no matter what Bob's politics were, he cared

about the troops and he spent many holidays away from his family to entertain the men and women in uniform. I expressed my gratitude to her. She surprised the heck out of Mimi and me by telling me that she admired me and told me to keep up doing what I am doing, that it is "important work."

The night that I went to see the four women peace activists, I met two of them: Betty Williams from Ireland, who helped in the Irish peace process, and Jody Williams, an American who got 150 countries to sign a resolution to stop using land mines. (The United States has not signed it.) Betty told me that many women Nobel laureates around the world are lobbying to have me nominated for the Nobel Peace Prize for 2006. The direction that my life has taken is amazing to me. Me? Nominated for the Nobel Peace Prize? If you look at my high school yearbook, underneath my senior picture, it should say: Cindy Miller, least likely to grow up to be Cindy Sheehan.

When I was speaking to Betty and Jody, I saw the same commitment and urgency for peace in them that I know in myself. I know that I have already done so much and sacrificed so much for peace, but I always feel that I should be doing more. I literally believe that I would do almost anything for peace. At the moment, I am trying to figure out what would be the best way to prevent the upcoming invasion of Iran. I have been in deep discussions with Daniel Ellsberg, who helped stop the killing in the Vietnam War by exposing the Pentagon Papers. We are trying to figure out what we need to do to stop the insanity. I really hope and pray that by the time this book is published the Bush administration has not already taken the cataclysmic, insane step of bombing Iran.

I really think that, as of this writing, George Bush is out of his mind and out of control. I hope by the time my book comes out that George Bush will have had to resign in disgrace—or will have been impeached and removed from office by a Congress that finally grew some balls. George is the only president ever who has admitted to crimes while in office, and he sits in his desk chair in the Oval Office free to commit even more crimes. If a prez can be impeached for a blow job, why can't one be impeached for lying to the country and for committing crimes against humanity?

I am disgusted with Congress for their seeming complicity in the transgressions of this administration. They nod their heads up and down with bobble-headed abandon and rubber-stamp anything that the Bush regime wants. Especially the Democrats, who should guard our freedoms and not allow the executive branch to steal them.

However, there are many men and women in our Congress whom I admire and count as friends. Maxine Waters from Los Angeles and Sheila Jackson Lee from Houston are two congresswomen who visited us at Camp Casey and always stand firm and speak loudly for peace and the rights of all Americans. I count them and Lynn Woolsey and Barbara Lee, both from Northern California, as my friends and corevolutionaries.

Representative Charlie Rangel from New York calls me his girlfriend and is an avid supporter of my work and has introduced a resolution in Congress praising my patriotism. When I was about to be arrested one time in front of the White House, he drove right up to stand in solidarity with all of us for peace. Charlie is a great proponent of bringing a fair conscription that would require public service, if not military service, for everyone, no matter what socioeconomic sphere a conscript comes from. I disagree with him because we know that the Bushes of the world will always get out of this. I don't believe in a draft, in any form.

When I met with Senator Ted Kennedy in his office for over an hour one day, I was honored and felt unworthy to be called by him "a true American hero and patriot." His office and his life are shrines to what it means to be an American and what true familial sacrifice is. Casey was born on JFK's birthday, and I can't imagine what it was like for Rose Kennedy having to bury four children. It is a monstrous thing to have to endure burying one child. No matter what you say about the Kennedy clan, they have given more to this country than any family that I can think of. Ted Kennedy does not have to be a senator. He doesn't have to put up with the constant shit that he encounters, but he has always been a strong advocate for the people of the USA and for his own constituents and he has lived his political career from a true progressive center. I admire Ted Kennedy more than any other senator currently serving.

When I met with the junior senator from Massachusetts,

John Kerry, I was unimpressed and I have not been impressed with him since. He tried to convince me that he spoke out strongly against the war during the campaign. Only recently, because the polls have shown support for bringing the troops home, has he spoken out stridently against George's cruelty in Iraq. I predict he will run for president again and is trying to be an anti-Hillary. I am sorry I supported John Kerry in 2004 because he was not antiwar, just anti–how Bush was handling it. I don't want a president who thinks that any war can be competent or smartly fought. I will not support him or Hillary if they are the Democratic nominees—I will support any candidate who is antiwar—anti-*all*-war.

When I met with Senator Clinton along with Senate Minority Leader Harry Reid, I believed that I, Dede, and another Gold Star mom, Lynn Bradach, whose son Travis Nall was KIA in Iraq, were making headway with our stories of pain and loss. Senator Reid said as he left the meeting that he had "no choice" but to support us. Well, he hasn't yet. We are still waiting.

But Hillary listened without replying for a long time. Then she said, "Well, what you all are doing is very important, but we need to keep the troops in Iraq to honor your loved ones' sacrifices!" I was stunned that a supposed progressive would say that. Also, I believe that the comment was calculatingly meant to hurt me, since I had already been speaking out against her wishy-washiness on the war. Hillary knew as well as anybody, and probably even better, that I had been demanding that George quit using Casey's sacrifice to justify more killing. I lost a lot of Hollywood support when I outed Hillary as a conservative in liberal clothing, but she is not a true progressive, and I believe that she would do anything for power—and we don't need another power-monger in the White House, no matter what party he or she belongs to.

My all-time-favorite congressman is John Conyers, who invited me to testify in June at his Downing Street Memo hearings. He has committed his life to serving this country, and he does the right thing after much study and consideration. John Conyers has a lifelong supporter in me.

From meeting governmental dignitaries and celebrities like Michael Moore and Meg Ryan, to receiving awards and praying with religious leaders of all faiths, to walking with Thich Nhat Hahn and kissing Paul Newman, to spending New Year's Eve with Graham Nash and his lovely family and talking politics with stars from *The West Wing,* my life has in some ways become a dreamlike sequence of incredible events.

I believe the pinnacle of far-fetched episodes that have swirled into my life was the night that I was "headlining" a fund-raiser for my friends Peter Dudar and Sally Marr, who made an incredible film called *Arlington West,* which they use for counterrecruitment efforts and which my family and I are featured in.

One of the musical guests that night was Jackson Browne. I am Jackson Browne's number one fan, no matter what Dede or anyone says. I have resonated with and loved his music seemingly forever. From the first song I heard by him, "Doctor My

Eyes," to his recently rereleased *Lives in the Balance,* which shows a sign that says MEET WITH CINDY in its new video, I have taken his lyrics and music into my heart and they have become part of me. I couldn't even listen to his music for over a year after Casey was killed because it was so emotionally powerful to me. (Besides, I have always thought he was so hot!)

After my talk, when I got to meet him and had him in a death grip of a hug that I never wanted to end, he told me, "You are an amazing woman and an amazing communicator." I can't decide which was the better compliment, Jackson's or Dario's, but I don't care. I'll take both of them.

Becoming a "peace icon" is hard and dangerous work. I shrink back a little when I hear that I am sometimes called that, because we all know what often happens to peace icons: They are killed violently. I know that I will die eventually, no escaping that, and when I do I will be reunited with Casey, so I am not afraid and I am willing to put my life on the line for the Noble Cause of Peace. Peace and justice are the only noble causes worth fighting for.

But let's face it, I also lead a very fascinating and exciting life with rewards and benefits. However, the good things that happen always happen under a dark cloud. I would probably not be doing what I am doing if Casey hadn't been killed. It is so hard to let myself enjoy the pleasures and satisfactions of my current life, to let go and let life unfold for the better after it slammed me in the gut with the death of my firstborn.

But when I got to meet my number one hero, Jackson

Browne, to hug him and receive an amazing compliment that was so meaningful to me, I did let myself accept it and enjoy it.

Casey and my other children cut their teeth on Jackson Browne records. He was a pervasive presence in our home, always, always.

When I met Jackson, I felt Casey in a group hug with us, whispering in my ear: "Way to go, Mom. Way to go." I felt like Casey had given me an early birthday or Christmas present from Heaven.

Epilogue

I AM WRITING THE FINAL WORDS TO MY BOOK ON April 4, 2006, sitting on my son's grave.

It is a bitterly cold day here in Vacaville, California, in sharp contrast to the lovely warm spring day when Casey was killed exactly two years ago.

If I still believed in the God of my past, I would invite Him (the God of my past was a Him) down to sit next to me under this angry April sky and ask Him one simple question: "Why?"

The God of my past was omniscient, so He would know what I meant:

"Why did You take such a wonderful human being when he was so young, and why did You do it so violently?

"Why are You punishing me and my family?

"Why are You punishing our country with this fool of a president who claims to get his marching orders for war from You?

"Why are You sacrificing me on the altar of peace?"

235

It doesn't do any good just to ask questions—I must seek the answers for myself from the universal godness in all of us.

I reflect on the fact that two years ago, I would have looked up at the sky and screamed "Why, why, why!" with fresh rage and raw pain. Now I ask the question with a rage that has been gone over with a fine-tooth comb, that ebbs and flows with the continuing and constant barrage of fresh crimes against America and crimes against humanity that emanate from our nation's capital every day. It is now a dull pain that will be my constant companion until I die.

I must make friends with this pain that is not even absent when I sleep. I dream that I am grieving Casey and the awareness of my universe without him is the first thing that I think of when I wake up every morning and the last thing that I think of before I fall asleep. I must make friends with this pain—my constant companion. I wish I could divorce it, kill it, numb it, ignore it, forget about it, but I can't and I will never be able to.

The rage that I feel against an out-of-control Bush administration never even has a chance to cool. The black-hearted fascists who are still defending their sham war and are making a mockery of our rule of law in this country are constantly throwing the fact that they are cold-blooded killers with a total disregard for humanity into our collective, gullible American faces.

I have already answered the question that I posed to God.

I am doing this so my son will never be forgotten. Buddhists say a person dies twice: once when his or her body dies and once when the last person who remembers him or her dies. Casey will never die. He will be immortal, like the superheroes in the comics and action figures that he collected.

I am also doing this to retrieve our naïve American souls from the soul stealers who don't come in the dead of night, but steal our souls in broad daylight with no remorse.

Afterword

The Struggle Continues

THE FINAL CHAPTER OF THE BOOK IS NOT WRITTEN, and as a matter of fact, it cannot be written.

My life is not over, but more important, Casey's life is not over. Casey will live on forever in the movement that his dying created.

All of our children who died in this unfortunate chapter of American history will never be forgotten, because I pledge that their deaths will always count for lasting and true peace.

We will continue to reach across borders to forge the bonds that tie the human race together. We will hold our leaders accountable for killing our brothers and sisters and prevent them from demonizing other members of our human family to justify more killing.

This was a story of love and hope for the future. It is a continuing struggle for peace and justice for the world and for our children.

I am and will be forever ashamed that my apathy partially led to my son's death, and I take full responsibility for my lack of education and ignorance. I will be saying my mea culpas forever for allowing my son to march off to an illegal and immoral war.

I am mostly sorry that I bought into the lie that one person cannot make a difference. One person can make a difference. I am living proof of that.

I did something so simple on August 6, 2005. Anyone can do what I did on that scorchingly hot August day . . . I sat down. One simple person changed history with a simple act.

I hope this book has been a challenge to everyone who thinks that one person can't make a difference. That one voice is insignificant and minor. That one vote is wasted.

I hope this book has been a challenge to you to make your dash have meaning.

Go now and change the world. It is in us all.

These are the last words written for this book.

However, the story is just beginning.

How You Can Get Involved:
A Resource Guide

ONLINE RESOURCES

Gold Star Families for Peace: www.gsfp.org

G.I. Rights Hotline/Conscientious Objectors:
www.girights.objector.org

Iraq Veterans Against the War: www.ivaw.net

Veterans for Peace: www.veteransforpeace.org

War Resisters League: www.warresisters.org

CODEPINK Women for Peace: www.codepinkalert.org

United for Peace and Justice: www.unitedforpeace.org

Guerrero Azteca Project: www.guerreroazteca.org

American Friends Service Committee: www.afsc.org

Mothers Against the Draft: www.mothersagainstthedraft.org

Peace Action: www.peace-action.org

National Priorities Project: www.nationalpriorities.org

Truthout: www.truthout.org

SUGGESTED READING

War Is a Racket, by General Smedley D. Butler (Feral House, 2003 [repr.]).

How to Stop the Next War Now: Effective Responses to Violence and Terrorism, edited by Jodie Evans and Medea Benjamin (Inner Ocean Publishing, 2005). A collection of antiwar essays by notable women working for peace around the world.

The Power of Nonviolence: Writings by Advocates of Peace, edited by Howard Zinn (Beacon Press, 2002).

War Resisters League Organizer's Manual, by the War Resisters League (War Resister's League, 1986 [rev. ed.]).